The Last Voyage of the Jean F. Anderson

The three-masted schooner *Jean F. Anderson* in the La Have River, Nova Scotia, probably in the late 1930s. The *Anderson* had a distinctive color scheme: a white hull with black rail. (Photo by Knickle's Studio, Lunenburg, Nova Scotia)

The Last Voyage of the Jean F. Anderson

Charles H. Turnbull

Mystic Seaport Museum, Inc.
Mystic, Connecticut
1990

Copyright 1990 by Mystic Seaport Museum, Inc.
All Rights Reserved

Cataloging in Publication Data

Turnbull, Charles H. 1923-
        The last voyage of the Jean F. Anderson.
Mystic, Connecticut, Mystic Seaport Museum, Inc., 1990.
        105 p. illus. 23 cm.
        1. Seafaring Life. 2. Coastwise
        Navigation. 3. Merchant Ships.
        4. Schooners.
        G540.T8
ISBN: 0-913372-55-2

Designed by Terry A. Rutledge
Typeset in Trump Mediaeval; display face is Present Script
Printed by McNaughton & Gunn, Ann Arbor, Michigan

Manufactured in the United States of America

To My Valiant Shipmates

Contents

1. I Must Go Down to the Sea   11

2. Georges Bank   22

3. New York: A Poor Relation
    Through the Front Door   54

4. Light to the S'uth'ard   70

5. Moonstruck   84

6. The Vessel's True Master   88

7. Ghosts   101

Illustrations

The *Jean F. Anderson*   Frontispiece

The author   10

The *Jean F. Anderson*, ready for launch   16

Layout of the forward house   25

View of the forecastle   27

Detail of typical schooner masthead gear   38

Captain St. Clair Geldert   45

Crew of the *Jean F. Anderson*   46

The author and Mate Bill Snow   46

The *Jean F. Anderson* in Newtown Creek   59

The author on the jibboom   62

View of the *Jean F. Anderson* from the jibboom   64

The helmsman's view of the *Jean F. Anderson*   76

The author's Certificate of Discharge   97

The *Jean F. Anderson* in port   102

The author in his seagoing garb. In this view, looking aft on the deck of the *Anderson*, the forward house is at left. (Author's photo)

I Must Go Down to the Sea

It seemed like forever that I had been telling my parents I was going to go to sea. They knew I had been reading everything that I could find about sailing vessels and voyages to the South Seas and that I spent as much time messing around small boats and sailing them as I could. But my parents knew, too, that I was well enmeshed in the business of getting an education and that life at sea was not compatible with what they had in mind for my future. They just said, "Sure," knowing that it wouldn't work. Deep inside I knew it, too.

But in 1941 it happened. Canada was at war. As in many a previous July, I had sailed from New York to Yarmouth, Nova Scotia, in the Eastern Steamship Lines' *Acadia*. On the drive up from Yarmouth to the family's summer cottage at Smith's Cove I spied an old four-master aground on the beach at Meteghan. Nothing would do but to stop and, it being low tide, walk around her weathered grey hull. Her paint was mostly gone, but her name, *Reine Marie Stewart*, was clearly readable on her transom. Surely it was a tragedy that she lay there unused, abandoned and unloved. I lay both hands up on her towering rough sides as though in homage and also to receive some intangible essence. What a pity; what a waste. If she lay there, was I too late to taste firsthand the tail end of the age of sail?

Smith's Cove seemed dead to me after finishing my freshman year at Wesleyan University in Connecticut. Most Americans had stayed away from this resort area because of the new war, and most Canadian men from the age of eighteen up were involved in something more serious than taking the summer off and having fun.

One evening soon after I arrived I announced to my mother and grandmother that I was off to sea and would leave after breakfast the next morning. The ladies were upset, but gave me little argument. I conceded that they could drive me as far as Milford and leave me at the end of the Victory Road.

Aside from what I wore, my kit consisted of an extra shirt, pants, one pair of undershorts, two pairs of cotton socks, toothbrush, toothpaste, shaving things, a second pair of sneakers, a light wool sweater and a sorry-looking rain jacket that was no longer waterproof. These I rolled up inside a thin sleeping bag and the old moss-colored blanket that we used on picnics down at Sandy Cove. I tied it all up with clothesline, using two loops as shoulder straps.

The day was fair and the pack light. I could have walked the whole distance to Lunenburg, but that wasn't necessary. Soon a friendly woodsman gave me a lift as far as he went in his pounding stake-bed truck. And then there were others.

There was no empty berth to be found in Lunenburg. Fishing, I found out, was like marriage. It wasn't to be entered into lightly or unadvisedly, and it required a long courtship. I had a good look at the famous old *Bluenose* tied up at the wharf. She was only recognizable to me because of the name, clearly legible on her starboard bow. Other than that she bore no resemblance to the legendary fisherman on the back of the dime and on thousands of calendars and post cards. Her topmasts were gone and her tall spars were cut short – "spike spars" they called them. Where I always pictured the helmsman gripping the wheel, clad in dripping oilskins and sou'wester, was a large box of a wheelhouse. There was no gleaming canvas – only a grey leg-o-mutton sail rigged to the foremast. It was streaked and blotched with rust, coal dust and grease. The vessel needed paint desperately, and her gear lay where it had fallen. She appeared unloved and deserted. Powerful but smelly diesel engines had displaced her beautiful sails and had caused her rigging to shrivel. This was an act of treason in my idealistic mind. All this was to me a severe disappointment and a shattered ideal.

On the north side of the wharf where the *Bluenose* lay was a schooner that was bound for Barbados the following day. As up was to down, was this four-masted vessel, the *Lillian E. Kerr*, to the disfigured *Bluenose*. She already had a full crew, but one of the men told me there was another vessel in Bridgewater that would soon be sailing, bound for Jamaica. I ached that I had been too late to sign on for the Barbados trip and feared I would be out of luck in Bridgewater, too. Nevertheless, I made good time getting up there to find out.

On the left bank of the La Have River, just below the bridge at Bridgewater, lay the three-masted schooner *Jean F. Anderson*. Her port of registry in black letters on the transom was La Have, N.S. She wasn't as elegant as the four-master I had seen in Lunenburg, but nonetheless I loved her instantly. Her paint was not bright, and she appeared smothered by a deckload of bright, fragrant spruce furring.

Yes, they were shorthanded, needing two more in the crew. No, they didn't mind that I was a greenhorn. Captain St. Clair Geldert, a short, square-built man in a striped engineer's cap, stained brown with sweat around the band, and grubby yellow suspenders, squinted suspiciously up at me through thick, black-rimmed glasses and asked me where I was from. "Smith's Cove," I lied. I didn't want the fact that I was an American to prevent me from getting this berth. Another squint, this time all over, and a puckering of the lips. I had time to watch the sunlight glinting on the white stubble on his pink jaw and chin.

"The wessel needs a man if he don't sojer none," he said. I understood the Lunenburg substitution of "w" for "v" and it always made me want to smile, but I had no clue as to the meaning of the verb "sojer." (Years later I found out that the word was a corruption of "soldier" and reflected the lazy and drunken tendencies of British military men at the time of the American Revolution.)

I must have said the right thing when I said, "Count on me," for the captain replied, "Come along," and we walked right away up to the customhouse. There he learned my real address and nationality. It didn't matter; I was signed on as ordinary seaman. I was to be paid at the rate of $20.00 a month, payable when I signed off. This would be at Jacksonville, Florida, so that I could get back to Wesleyan for the start of the fall term.

The cargo of lumber was destined for New York. We were to sail in two days. Before returning to the vessel I sent a post card to my mother to tell her what I was doing, the name of the vessel, where she was bound, what the cargo was and the date of sailing.

Deck seams needed caulking and we did those that were not covered by the deck cargo. Harry, who was to be my watch-mate on the captain's watch, caulked the seams with oakum, pounding it in tightly with a mallet and caulking iron. I ran between the driftwood fire, which was built between rocks on the shore beyond the wharf, and the seam on the deck with a pot of melted pitch. The captain told me to be quick about it and I was. I was so quick I became careless and tripped. The hot pitch soaked my right pant-leg from knee to ankle. Fortunately I wasn't burned, but that part of my pants remained stiff as a shingle for the whole trip. In the meantime the mate and Frenchy, the other man in the fo'c's'le, were busy replacing some running rigging that was not rugged enough for another trip at sea.

Only the cook, Ross Peeler, stood no watch, but he was always available when needed. The other five men were divided into two watches: the captain's and the mate's. We sailed one man shorthanded, including a greenhand to boot.

The vessel was a tern schooner, measuring 140 feet from stem to stern along the deck, 33.3 feet across the beam, drawing 12.6 feet, and with a volume of 396 tons. She was unusual in having a long poop deck that extended forward to the mainmast. Her main deck thus became a short well deck.

The designation "tern" had nothing to do with the raucous little seabirds with forked tails that dart and wheel faster and more joyously than gulls. It comes from the Latin "terni," meaning "three each." With its many small ports, Nova Scotia had come to rely upon these medium-sized schooners with three masts to carry local cargoes of raw materials to the outside world. Schooners with two masts carried fishermen and fish.

The *Jean F. Anderson*, ready for launch at Port Wade, Nova Scotia, 1919. (Courtesy Admiral Digby Museum, Digby, Nova Scotia)

The *Jean F. Anderson* had been built at Port Wade, Nova Scotia, near Digby, in 1919 at the end of the World War I shipbuilding boom. Even when most of her sister schooners were laid up for want of trade by the Great Depression, the *Anderson* was kept under sail by the Publicovers of La Have, Nova Scotia, running cargoes like pulpwood to the United States and salt back from the Caribbean to Nova Scotia. Now she had just been bought by a Captain Reid of Crossroads, Jamaica, for $15,000, a high price for an old tern schooner.

Captain Reid must have had his eye set on profits to be made during the war because of the diversion of shipping from the Caribbean to the supplying of a besieged and beleaguered Europe. Captain Reid, a swarthy young man in a business suit, was there the day we sailed. He had loaded two large diesel engines into the hold before the lumber was put into her. They were to be installed after arriving in Jamaica. The cost of installation was lower in Jamaica than in Nova Scotia. To get us to that tropical island, however, we had only sails – eleven of them – to propel us. There were two other engines in her and they were a tremendous help, but they didn't turn propellers. They were single-cylinder make-and-break gasoline engines, one for pumping the bilge and one to weigh anchor and hoist the three largest sails. The mate was the only one to touch them. He used the one by the mainmast to pump the bilge at eight o'clock every morning.

We sailed with the outgoing tide about five o'clock in the evening. A small tug took our hawser and slowly pulled us the ten miles downriver past the town of La Have at the river's mouth. As there was no wind, we remained in tow five miles out into the Atlantic Ocean to the east of Moser Island. After passing La Have the mate got the donkey (hoisting) engine

going and we got sail on her. First the mainsail, then the foresail, the spanker, the forestaysail, the inner jib, the outer jib
and the flying jib. It would have been heavy work indeed without the engine. Even with the mechanical advantage of the
man-powered capstan on the foredeck we would not have had
enough beef among us to do as good and as quick a job. I was
thankful for this ponderous engine, and I hoped that it would
always start obediently when the mate wanted it to.

In the feverish activity of making sail there was no time
to think about wind. No other sounds could have struck my
ears with greater romantic impact at that moment than those
of hoisting the sails: the slow chug-chug-skip of the engine; the
squealing of dozens of blocks, each with a slightly different
pitch; the creaking of the gaff and boom jaws against the mast;
and the clank and rattle of the boom tackles. There was no
time to stop and watch and listen. The handling of the lines
and sails didn't allow it, but the work and the sounds blended
into a time-honored dance with as blood-stirring an accompa-
niment as the skirl of the bagpipes and the booming of the
bass drum.

The tension on the halyards was so great that they
seemed like oak bars instead of flexible sisal rope. I was wondering how we could get them belayed and still keep that
tension. Never mind. The mate had a "stopper," a short piece
of rope with a stout steel hook on one end, that solved this
problem. He hooked this piece of rope onto the eye of the
halyard footblock on the deck and with the other end he tied a
rolling hitch onto the vertical part of the halyard. With the
halyard thus precariously and temporarily secured, we took the
turns off the donkey engine capstan and the line out of the
snatch blocks that led it there, keeping as much tension as

possible, and transferred it to the belaying pin on the pin rail.

When the first four sails were set the tug slowed and cast off our hawser. While Harry and I hauled in the line we caught glimpses of the tug heading back toward La Have. Only after the flying jib was set did I notice that the vessel was gently rolling in a ground swell, and that the faintest breath of breeze was beginning to smooth out the wrinkles in the sails. We were underway. As the sun set over the land, the lighthouse on West Ironbound Island blinked good-bye, and a grey, empty sea lay ahead.

I had but a few seconds for reflection upon the rapid succession of events and to observe my new surroundings before the captain said, "Well, Charlie, it's time you learn to steer." He showed me the course on the compass in the kerosene-lit binnacle. "Now don't keep looking at the compass. Keep your eye on the wessel's head and line it up with a point. When you see her head start to get off course stop her right away. If you was watching the compass you'd get way off before you'd notice. Check with the compass once in a while."

I didn't see then how you could be sailing straight out to sea and still aim for a point. I thought all "points" were on land and that everything at sea was moving, liquid, undependable.

There wasn't long to wonder about it before the motion of the vessel riding the ground swell got to my stomach. I always believed I was immune to seasickness, so I was astonished and mortified. The captain came to the rescue and took the wheel while I heaved a small meal over the taffrail to the fish. With them fed I felt somewhat better. "You'll get used to it," he said. "I know a captain, an old man now, who got sick every time he went to sea. It was always the same – just for

the first hour or so, even if it was calm. Then after that no gale
of wind could get to him."

By now it was mercifully eight bells and time to change
the watch and go forward for supper. At the mention of supper
all thoughts of seasickness fled, and I realized I was starved.
Hard work, fresh air, excitement and youth make a ferocious
appetite. In the footsteps of countless predecessors, my brief
encounter with mal de mer was concluded, never to return.
Only from the vantage point of many decades does this sudden
change of heart take on an additional meaning: Man must work
to eat and eat to survive. That is Man's basic relationship, the
foundation upon which all civilization must stand.

The post card that I had written in Bridgewater reached
my mother the day we sailed. I had no idea how much anguish
it would cause her. Because of the need to keep this kind of
strategic information from the Germans, someone in the
Bridgewater post office had censored it, and a thorough job it
was. All vital words had been cut out with a razor blade, leaving only slots. The card read:

> Dear Mom,
>   I am shipping out on the (slot). We sail
> (slot). We are bound for (slot) with a cargo of
> (slot). From there we go to (slot). I'll sign off there.
>   Love, Charles

The impact and significance of the war suddenly struck
home to my mother. Having no idea where her darling boy
might be or might end up, she and my grandmother immediately drove across the province in pursuit. There was a fair-
haired boy to be rescued.

Inquiring at the customhouse (at least the censor hadn't cut out the postmark) my mother was told that she could see the vessel being towed downstream if she hurried. Realizing that she was no threat to the war effort or to the safety of the merchant marine, the customs officer filled in the blanks on the post card for her. Thus she was able to notify my father in New Jersey to expect me in New York in about a week.

Georges Bank

During the first few days at sea, powerful new impressions and experiences came at me in quick succession. It was a jumble, but the jumble got sorted out without any accident or damage, and I quickly became a sailor. Life at sea was not the romantic idyll described by John Masefield. It was different; it was hard; it was elemental.

We worked watch-and-watch. That's the only way we could have managed with such a small crew. The day was divided into five periods (watches) of four hours each and two of two hours (the dog watches.) We would be on watch, say, from 8:00 A.M. to noon, then 4:00 P.M. to 6:00, then 8:00 P.M. to midnight, then 4:00 A.M. to 8:00, thus standing watch for twelve hours a day. The two dog watches served to alternate the crew between two schedules, thus being fairer to all. But being on watch a total of twelve hours a day was not the whole of a day's work. Between 8:00 A.M. and 8:00 P.M., except on Sundays and at mealtimes, those not on watch had to work. There was always scraping, painting, mending or some other maintenance work to be done. So, added to the twelve hours on watch were six more hours of work to be performed six days a week. All told that made 516 hours a month. At my rate of $20.00 a month, I was working for 3.88 cents per hour. That didn't include those times of emergency when all hands had to turn out in the middle of the night to take in sail. The others in the crew were paid more, but I never found out how much. Frenchy and Harry were A.B.s (able-bodied seamen), and the captain, mate and cook were in a higher pay bracket than that, but none could look forward to retiring to enjoy great wealth.

Of course there were benefits that we received in excess of the actual pay in dollars. This nonspendable income was in the form of bed and board. Both of these aspects of life at sea in a sailing vessel are worth describing as they are not the same as would be encountered on shore.

The forecastle was the deckhands' quarters – a lofty name, but certainly no relation to a castle of any kind. Its correct pronunciation, "fo'c's'le," cut it down to size and eliminated any suggestion of grandeur. It was our bedroom, dining room and refuge. It was a small dark room on the starboard side of the deckhouse, and just aft of the donkey-engine room. On the port side of the deckhouse, and the same size as the fo'c's'le, was the galley. The deckhouse was built as far forward as possible. In each of the rooms a portion of the foremast protruded. Forward of the house was the raised fo'c's'le deck with the hand-powered capstan, the chain locker and then the stem itself.

Between the galley and the fo'c's'le was the pie-hole through which the cook passed us our meals and retrieved our dirty dishes. He would scold us with "Don't fress so bad," when we spilled. I chuckled to myself about his use of the German word "fressen," meaning the kind of eating that animals do, instead of "essen," the way humans eat. Apparently these verbs distinguish, too, the civilized from the savage. Afterwards he would pass us a damp rag to mop up the originally white oilcloth (true oilcloth, no plastic then) on top of our mess table, which was attached to the bulkhead below the pie-hole.

Four wooden bunks – two uppers and two lowers – were built into the starboard bulkhead of the fo'c's'le. They measured six feet long and about two feet wide, and were fitted with burlap ticks half-filled with straw. Above each top bunk was a tiny window about nine inches high and eighteen inches wide. Being the junior member of the crew, I got a top bunk. I chose the one nearest the door, so I had plenty of fresh air. I kept my window open all the time except when rain or spray came in. The smallest coal stove I could imagine was secured close to the foremast. We never used it. Shivering some raw nights on Georges Bank I shuddered to think how uncomfortable winter might be. My shipmates never tired of competing in telling tales of winter storms at sea.

Our little home measured just six feet by twelve feet – table, bench, bunks and baby coal stove included. We hung our oilskins on pegs just forward of the table where their dripping would bother nobody. We entered the room from the aft side through a sliding door with a sill about sixteen inches high. This sill kept things fairly dry inside when we were running in heavy weather and there was much water sloshing about on the deck outside, but it also made it hard to sweep our quarters clean. While I was in the vessel the fo'c's'le was never swept, but Frenchy kept it clean by occasionally dashing several buckets of seawater into the far corners when the vessel was on the port tack. Before doing this he would pull the plug from the scupper in the starboard after corner to allow the water

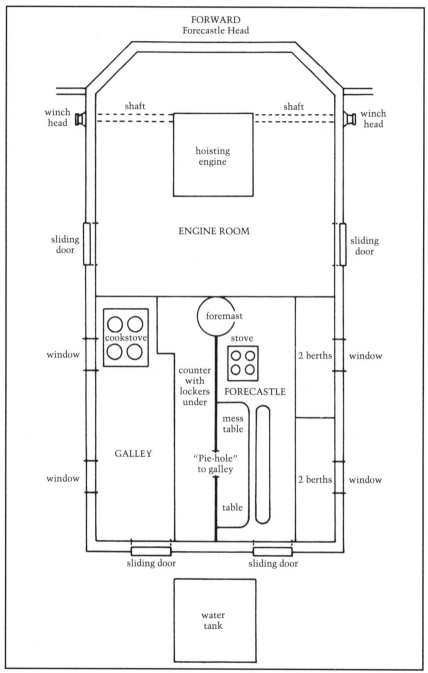

Layout of the *Jean F. Anderson*'s forward house, as remembered by the author. Drawn by Irene Bucacci.

with its burden of dirt to drain out.

The captain, mate and cook had tiny staterooms aft in the after house. Each of these cells opened into a large room with a table in it. Here the captain laid out his charts and plotted the ship's course. Also at this table the captain and the mate ate their meals. Punctually and faithfully, the cook carried their food and clean dishes back aft to them from the galley. No matter what the weather, and no matter how violently the vessel pitched and was swept by the tops of waves that were ripped from their foundations by strong winds, the cook delivered the meals on time. Although he was sure-footed and cautious, he carried everything suspended in a bucket. This prevented spilling and was especially effective with soup. As he held the handle away from his body, the bucket's center of gravity was always directly below his hand. There were times, however, when the captain and the mate had their soup diluted with a touch of rain from the sky or brine from the deep.

Although there was ample room for the rest of us to eat in the after house, tradition and the maintenance of good ship's discipline demanded the separation of the crew from the officers. So rigid was this discipline that on the rare occasions when Frenchy, Harry or I entered the after house we had to remove our hats. Tradition and discipline also required the three of us underlings to stay on the lee side of the vessel whenever we had to be on the after deck. The windward side was reserved for the captain alone. This perhaps became tradition when captains wanted to avoid the odors of the unwashed bodies of the crew. Uncontaminated air was always available to windward. The crew, however, passing to his lee could smell the captain. In the case of the *Jean F. Anderson* and of Captain Geldert, we all smelled quite normal and none of us was of-

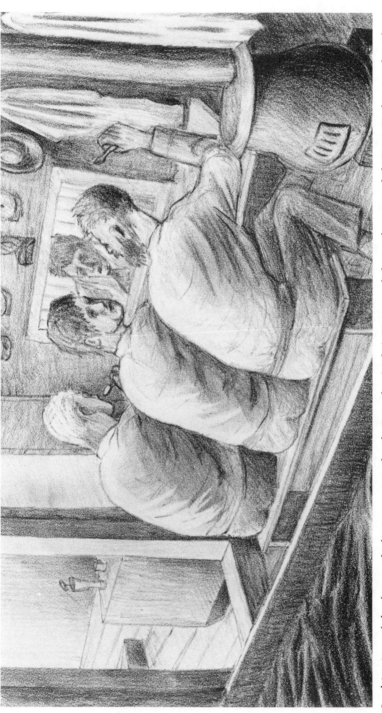

In this view of the forecastle from an upper bunk, Frenchy (*right*), Harry and the author eat while Ross Peeler watches them through the pie-hole. Outside is the water tank. The author recorded his impression of the *Anderson's* forecastle in this lithograph in 1942.

fensive. At least this is what we believed to such a degree that there was never a comment or shrug about it.

As we all ate the same diet, we all produced odors that were much the same. Individual metabolisms made slight differences, but I never paid attention to this. Smoking and chewing tobacco made more of a difference. The cook, Harry and Frenchy smoked cigarettes, and the mate chewed tobacco. I tried chewing tobacco for a while, and when I did I noticed that the mate lost any distinguishing odor that he had beforehand. I assume that he and I shared an odor that was noticeable to the others, but which, as we shared it, cancelled out in each other's senses. As we all were out in the fresh air so much of the time with the breeze whipping through our clothes, most odors were whisked away downwind. But what's a little body smell between shipmates?

Although the ship's officers always ate first and in comparative splendor, we deckhands ate better. Not only was our food warmer, having had to travel only the four feet from the galley stove to our table, but it never ran the risk of being diluted by rain or seawater. I suspect, too, that we had a greater abundance of it, as the cook ate with us, he on the galley side of the pie-hole and we on ours.

Ross Peeler, the cook, was an expert seaman from Riverport, Nova Scotia. He had been going to sea for ten years. He was a handsome twenty-five-year-old with a ready smile and a twinkle in his eye. He was always soft-spoken and considerate and made me feel that I had always been his friend. His father had cooked on fishing vessels for years, and everyone in the Peeler family learned to cook and bake. In the late twenties his father and mother had taken their four children to Lake Worth, Florida. His mother had a stroke there at the age of thirty. His father did odd jobs until the Depression drove the family back home to Riverport in 1930. Then, at fifteen years of age, Ross started his career at sea. He sailed on schooners as able-bodied seaman. He went out fishing on the Grand Banks, first on "salt fishermen" then on "fresh fishermen." With his experience as deckhand, fisherman and cook, Ross was a valuable man to have in any vessel.

As we ate, Ross watched us carefully. Once I reached for the molasses to put on my already-buttered bread. He stopped me as I touched the jug. "Either butter or molasses, not both. That's the rule."

Usually when we asked for more he would oblige and the food came steaming from the stove. Sometimes though he would say, "Uh-uh, de soup is all."

The other advantage we had over the officers was the warmth from the cookstove that came through the pie-hole. This was especially appreciated on the trip from Bridgewater to New York. It was relief from the cold, often wet, watches on deck. There was no heat back in the after house. The captain would not use coal for this purpose in summer, no matter what the temperature. Coal was for cooking. Anything else was waste, and waste of any kind was unconscionable.

There was no ice or mechanical refrigeration in the *Jean F. Anderson*. No commercial sailing vessel of that era had these frills. Consequently, the cook's choice of foods was limited mainly to the old standard ship's stores items. As we were traveling coastwise and were not scheduled to be at sea for long periods, some fruits and vegetables could be included.

Before leaving Bridgwater the cook brought aboard a tub of butter, which he allowed to warm up. When it was soft he worked an extra pound of salt into it, even though it had been previously salted at the dairy. He said it was to keep the butter from going rancid. It also had another advantage from the viewpoint of the captain; it made us use less of it. Our bodies seemed to tell us when we had consumed enough salt; beyond that we wanted no more.

Our diet was heavy on potatoes with some cabbage, carrots and turnips thrown in. The meat was the lowest grade of salt beef with a high percentage of gristle in it. There was also salt cod and salt pork. The latter was used only once a week as an ingredient in the Saturday supper baked beans. These were the best beans I had ever tasted, made with plenty of molasses and powdered mustard. The cook always made enough for us to have them again the following day – one of the blessings of the Sabbath.

There was bread aplenty. It was fresh and tasty, probably the envy of many a struggling housewife. Usually it was white, but sometimes it had molasses and left-over oatmeal in it. This was a special treat, but with either butter or molasses, not both.

The first time I saw the "pancakes" that the cook turned out I didn't realize I would soon consider them, too, to be treats. They were made with a very stiff batter and fried in more than enough fat. They measured three-quarters of an inch thick and were decidedly heavy. I have heard much less substantial pancakes referred to as "death wads." They were a mottled yellow and brown with crispy edges and glistened when they were hot. They were very filling, but tasted delicious with a little molasses; no butter was needed, they contained enough grease. The cook always made a lot of extra pancakes and stored them in the little cuddy locker in the fo'c's'le. They were welcome along with a mug of steaming tea when coming in from a chilly watch at midnight or at four in the morning. The cook always boiled the kettle and had hot tea ready at these times, but cold pancakes made the "mug-up" something special. The usual breakfast was oatmeal, plenty of it, tea with evaporated milk, bread, occasionally eggs and often oranges. No scurvy for this vessel's men.

Once or twice Ross baked a cake or cookies and served canned fruit – the height of shipboard luxury. As my father often said, "Thankit wi' little and canty wi' mair." [Thankful with little, overjoyed with more.]

Before we sailed from Bridgewater, the captain questioned me about my personal gear. He wouldn't think of me sailing with him without oilskins, but agreed that, as it was summer, I could get by without a sou'wester or rubber boots. So he bought me the longest oilskins, jacket and pants, that he could find in Lunenburg. He subtracted the $4.37 they cost from my pay when I signed off. I don't know how I would have fared without them. It did not take me long at sea to regret that he had not bought me rubber boots and a sou'wester, too.

As true oilskins disappeared from the scene years ago, I will describe them for you. The jacket was made of coarse unbleached muslin that had been doused in linseed oil and allowed to dry. It was lined with a lighter weight muslin and had a stand-up collar and a double flap down the front to keep water and wind from coming in around the buttons. The pants were very wide and were short-legged because rubber boots were normally worn under them. They had a high bib in front and shoulder straps. When new, oilskins were a lovely bright yellow, but they grew duller and picked up stains until they became a mottled tobacco color. From the beginning they had a tendency to leak slightly at the seams. With use this became more pronounced. After you had enough of this leaking, you would give them another coat of linseed oil and tie them in a small bundle for a day, so that the oil got into all the leaky places, and then hang them up to dry. They also tended to rot if not rinsed in fresh water as often as possible and hung in the rigging to get bone dry. If put away wet or salty, rot quickly started and the seams let go. Oilskins had another treacherous habit when rolled up with fresh oil on them. They would generate heat – occasionally enough to cause spontaneous combustion. They did turn aside wind and most of the wet, but the black rubber rainsuits that became available later are much warmer and drier.

For all their faults I was thankful for my new oilskins and wore them proudly. But even when I wore them, the rain soaked my head and ran down inside my collar. It wet my shirt and sweater from the elbows down. It soaked my pant-legs and feet from the knees down. Wet sneakers are never cozy, and are disgusting to pull on at midnight to face a cold, foggy watch on Georges Bank.

Rubber boots would have been my greatest comfort on the trip to New York. A sou'wester would have been my crowning luxury. Everybody else in the *Anderson* had good dependable Lunenburg sou'westers. They are always black and made like oilskins, but with a flannel lining and ear flaps that tie under the chin. They are distinguished from other sou'westers by the turned-up front that forms a gutter to divert water to the rear. In 1990 these are still being sold in stores that outfit fishermen. They look the same as the old ones, but the coating has been upgraded from the traditional linseed oil and lampblack to a safer and more dependable black vinyl plastic.

Before leaving Bridgewater I was annoyed that I was so tall and my bunk so short. I considered it my fault that I was six-foot-four rather than blaming the ship's builders for making the bunk only six feet long. The first rough night at sea, though, I became quite content with this discrepancy in sizes. If I curled up just right on my side and wedged myself in snugly, no motion of the vessel could budge me. I slept through the roughest conditions, but would awaken instantly if there was any change in the pattern of the ship's motion. If we changed course, or came about, or jibed, or if the wind picked up suddenly or died down, then I would be conscious just long enough to determine what was happening. Immediately afterwards I would resume the deep sleep that long hours of hard work, fresh air in abundance and youth demand. Soon enough would come the gruff, unwelcome voice saying, "Eight bells. Drop your _ _ _ _ _ and grab your socks." The watch below was never long enough.

Whether pleasant or not, going on watch at night was never dull. No matter what the weather and no matter how dark it was, there was always something to see. Also there was usually something to imagine. The shape of a wave, the motion of the vessel, the stars, the clouds, the moonlight, a finger of fog, something unidentified in the distance; all these gave rise to thought associations and the visualization of something the eyes did not actually see.

At night, my first night at sea under sail, leaving the dark loom of Nova Scotia behind was high adventure for me. There was a brief moment of panic when I turned and looked back at the low, black lumpiness of the land. No point of light twinkled anywhere, for Canada was at war and Maritimers knew how vital it was to maintain blackout. Maritimers all had men at sea.

The land looked more threatening than the cold, soulless sea ahead. For that moment I wondered whether there was any life or light or warmth or laughter or welcome hidden along that whole desolate-looking coast. Certainly there was none in the wet emptiness ahead, but neither were there lurking ledges or snarling breakers anywhere in the direction in which we were heading. At this point the sea became the vessel's friend and the hard, unyielding solid land became its enemy. I was suddenly aware that I was part of the vessel. Its friend became my friend and I adopted its enemies as well.

Plumbing and sanitary facilities in the *Jean F. Anderson* were primitive, but, as with most primitive things, completely trouble-free. Water was stored in a large steel tank bolted to the deck between the doorways of the fo'c's'le and the galley. This black cube measured four feet in each dimension and had a hand-operated pump stuck in the top. It held 500 gallons of fresh water. In addition to this there were three or four oak casks lashed to the top of the after house by the mizzenmast.

Urination was a simple matter, provided that you always did it over the lee rail and hung onto the shrouds with one hand. For more serious elimination the captain and mate had a hand-operated flush head in a little closet off the saloon in the after house. For us deckhands there was the old galvanized bucket with the broken rim in the engine room. It had twenty feet of line attached to it so that we could throw it over the side and dip up a few inches of water. There was never any inclination to linger over doing our jobs and never any thought of reading material to while away the time. This was the same all-purpose bucket that served to wash out the fo'c's'le, the galley and the deck. The officers urinated overboard by the mizzen shrouds; we deckhands did it by the fore shrouds. All were modest in the extreme and took care that their private parts were shielded from view. Having been accustomed to boys' camp and gym locker rooms, I did not understand such modesty.

There was a chipped white enameled mug on a heavy cord by the water tank. Harry and I brushed our teeth there once a day and spat overboard. Frenchy didn't brush because he had no teeth – not even false ones. Considering this lack, he ate heartily and without delay, and he spoke with amazing clarity. I supposed that this was because he had lost his teeth at an early age and had learned to compensate for their loss while still young. One day the mate, who never brushed at all and who had thick yellowish deposits connecting all his teeth, was in a talkative mood while I was performing this customary ritual. With a twinkle in his eye he said, "Charlie, you goin' ta scrub the 'nammel off." I don't remember him ever saying more than that unless it was connected with the work of the vessel. I doubt that mealtime conversation in the after house sparkled with wit, double entendre or loquacity. Even the normal, "Pass the butter," may have been dispensed with.

If the mate was a man of few spoken words, he had no written or printed words at his command at all. I wondered whether he was as helpless when confronted by numbers as he was by letters. Here we were at sea in an unarmed British vessel and the war in the North Atlantic was under way. The captain was elderly and none too robust. His poor vision was just sufficient to read the charts and to see the scale on the sextant. If he should fail and our mate find himself suddenly in command, would he be able to navigate? None of us others could handle the job.

We had no means of communication with other vessels or shore except voice – not even a megaphone. I assumed that the only course we could sail was west. Sooner or later it would fetch us up on some part of the North American coast. Maybe we would be lucky and get close enough to some other ship to ask them for a course to steer. At best, it would be the blindest kind of dead reckoning. The chances of making a landfall at a decent harbor were only a small fraction of the other possibilities, such as offshore ledges, low barrier islands, rocky headlands, unmarked sandbars, or downwind into a narrow unprotected bay. It would be better that the captain, with all his limitations, continue able to command. A good-natured, illiterate mate in command, though the finest seaman we had, might be a poor risk for a safe landfall.

While on watch we did one-hour tricks at the wheel. Every so often the captain would peer into the binnacle to see the compass reading, and then he would look behind at our wake. If he detected any lack of straightness to it and we were not sailing close-hauled, he had a sharp comment for the man at the wheel. This did not happen frequently on the trip to New York as the trip was up-wind all the way. Nearly always we were close-hauled.

Even my grandmother, who was born and raised in Gardiner, Maine, could not tell me why people in Maine and the Maritimes spoke of going up to Boston and then coming back down east again. With no words at all the vessel told me the answer. She was a painstaking teacher and taught lessons that could never be forgotten. Boston and New York lay upwind of Maine and Nova Scotia; it was a beat the whole way. Thus we went "up" to New York. A vessel returning to the Maritimes would go "down" home. The prevailing wind was from the southwest – from the direction of Boston and New York. Consequently, when being relieved at the wheel the helmsman would state the course to his replacement by saying, "By the wind." Any slight change in the wind direction either pushed our heading farther off the direct course to New York or improved it. If it put the vessel farther off course, the captain would usually have us bring the vessel about or jibe. It was a tedious process of gaining every possible inch to windward that we could.

Coming about, itself, was a tedious process. It was not at all like the light-as-a-feather, turn-on-a-dime, responding-in-seconds maneuver that I had grown used to in small sailboats. Nothing could have been simpler in the Snipes, Lightnings and Comets and other small boats I had excelled at sailing. The procedure on a tern schooner was slow and required a lot of climbing, running around and pulling on heavy running rigging. However, the principle is the same for all sailing vessels and craft.

A tern schooner, particularly one that is heavily laden, has a great deal of momentum. However, the large surface area of her hull slows her down rapidly when pointed into the wind, particularly in a rough sea. Often the momentum is insufficient to bring her around onto the other tack unless extra measures are taken – measures that probably would not occur to the yachtsman or racer of small craft.

When a schooner is brought about her jibs are left sheeted and are allowed to be taken aback so that they fill early and force the vessel's head off the wind onto the new tack. Then they are sheeted to leeward after their backing and turning function is no longer needed. Likewise, the forestaysail is backed, but in a different manner. Its tailrope is not touched

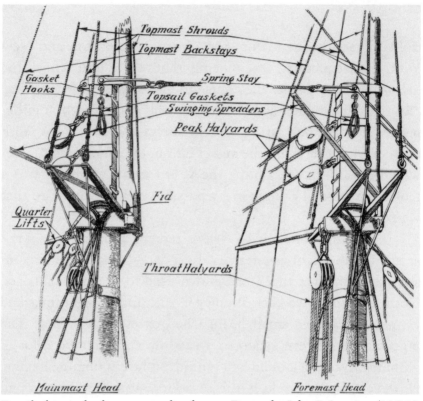

Detail of typical schooner masthead gear. Drawn by John F. Leavitt. (M.S.M. 76.1.31)

until the new tack has been achieved. Then the tailrope is released, the sail and its boom are allowed to swing to leeward on its traveler, and the tailrope is made fast to leeward. There is no need to touch the sheet. The foresail, being forward of the center of rotation amidships like the headsails, is also in a position to render a positive rotational force. It, too, is backed. To do this its boom tackle is not eased off and shifted to leeward until the bow is sufficiently around past the eye of the wind. When the wind is light and there is too much action of the main and spanker booms, their boom tackles are in use and must be eased off and shifted to the other side. These tackles are not used to back the mainsail or spanker in coming about. When the wind is steady and moderate, they are both made fast onto their own booms and are thus out of use.

Topsails add greatly to the complexity, work and time of bringing a schooner about. Before the maneuver was actually executed, the fore and main topsail halyards were eased a bit, and the fore and main tacks (the line from the bottom corner of the topsail to the deck) and fore and main topsail sheets were cast off. Second, the sail was clewed up with the clewline so that it became a loose, writhing creature just above the masthead. This was accomplished by hauling on the clewline, the most complicated line of all the running rigging. It acted somewhat like a purse string, gathering the three corners of the sail and the center of its belly loosely together at the masthead. However, since the halyard was still made fast, only the belly (the bunt), the lower corner (the tack) and after corner (the clew) were gathered in, effectively spilling the wind. The mizzen topsail did not need to be tended at this time.

Then, after the vessel was fully about on the new tack, a man would go aloft (I at the foremasthead) and move the clewed-up sail to leeward over the spring stay and topmast stay. He would then unhook the sheet, pass it under the spring stay and the topmast stay, and resecure it to the clew of the topsail, so that the sail could eventually fill to leeward without the danger of chaffing on the spring stay and topmast stay. He would then haul up the tack and drop it down to leeward of the peak halyard but to windward of the gaff. Someone on deck would sheet out the clew, then fully hoist the head with the halyard, and finally bring the tack around forward of the mast and make it fast to the lee pinrail. The procedure was simpler for the mizzen topsail because there was no spring stay or topmast stay to require the halyard, sheet or clewline to be handled – only the tack, and that was the last detail to be tended to in the labor-intensive, time-consuming processes of coming about. Topsail handling would have been a lot simpler and quicker if the topsail mast hoops, the spring stay and the masthead stay were not there and in the way. But these essential components of the rigging could not be eliminated. Even without topsails and topmasts, the spring stays must remain.

If the topsail was not to be reset, the halyard was also cast off before coming about and the whole sail clewed up to the masthead. After coming about it was then furled.

When we were making a series of short tacks and the added pulling power of the fore and main topsails was marginal, we would either leave the sail clewed up or partially clewed up. This latter arrangement left the sail hauled out by the sheet, but with tack pulled up and head pulled down. Thus we could ignore the fore and main topsails until we were again on a worthwhile course. This saved what a dear old Irish lady I knew later called "too much shiftin' o' the dishes fer the fewness o' the vittles."

The work involved in jibing (or wearing ship), changing tack by steering off the wind to get the wind on the other side, was considerably less, but it had two disadvantages. First, it was dangerous to make this maneuver except when the wind was light. Second, in jibing we went a little way downwind and lost some of the hard-won distance we had already made to windward. It made us that much farther from our destination. It did have the advantage for us at night on Georges Bank that no extra help was needed; two men could do it easily because no topsails were set.

In handling lines we were hampered by the deck load of lumber. In the dark and wet our footing was less than certain.

Ropes kept getting caught under the butt ends of boards. Although the lumber was carefully made fast with wire cables, chains and turnbuckles, many ends of boards had warped upwards enough to make footing difficult and tripping easy. We had rigged lifelines fore and aft over the top of the load, but they did not give the sense of security that came from the good solid chest-high rail of the well deck, pierced only by scuppers.

When the wind picked up and became too heavy for full sail, the topsails would be taken in first. This operation looked simple from the deck, but by the time we had to do this the sea had become quite rough and the job aloft more hazardous. The higher up the rigging we went, the more accentuated the vessel's motion became. By the time we reached the spreaders (crosstrees), where we stopped and worked, the motion was entirely different than it was on deck. It felt like being a small flag waved around in circles by a child watching a parade. I imagine riding a camel must give the same sensation, but with the circles smaller and with the distance to fall much less.

First the topsail was clewed up. Then, while standing on the spreaders we hugged the sail into a progressively smaller size and laced it with a gasket to the masthead. The upper end of the mast was square and had a series of hooks opening forward mounted on its aft face. In most schooners there was ordinarily a separate gasket to lace with, but we used the tack of the sail instead. Before the topsail was all bundled up it was far from tame, especially when wet. It fought against our straining to capture and confine it as though it were some wild beast. Occasionally it would surrender only after inflicting a torn and bleeding fingernail – something to remember it by. Work aloft with a topsail was a one-man job.

I had always heard and read, "One hand for the ship and

one hand for yourself." This advice may have applied to other ships and to other times, but it did not apply to the crew wrestling with the *Jean F. Anderson*'s whipping topsails. In our vessel it was "Both hands for the vessel. Hold on for yourself with your two feet and your ass." The latter just fitted securely between the two windward topmast shrouds that ran from the spreaders to the upper end of the topmast. Looking down from up there the deck looked hopelessly far away and small in the midst of the angry ocean. The deck appeared to be describing circles and was seldom directly beneath us, as the vessel was heeling over with the wind that was strong enough to make us shorten sail.

A fall from the spreaders could easily have resulted in a splash in the water rather than a thud on the deck. No doubt either would have been fatal. By the time the vessel could have been maneuvered to pick up the fallen sailor from the sea he would not be found. The vessel handled too sluggishly; the water would have been too rough and perhaps too dark. Furthermore, the cook and I were the only ones aboard who could swim.

With the topsails off her, the vessel would ride noticeably easier. They were so high above the water that they not only caught a greater velocity of wind, but they multiplied the heeling factor because they pressed on the upper ends of longer lever arms than did the three much larger sails below them. It was always a comfort to have the topsails securely lashed to the masthead and to be safely back to the relative stability and security of the deck. It was very lonely up there in a heavy wind at night.

When taking over the wheel while we were following a compass course rather than sailing by the wind I found it easy to select a point to steer toward when the sky was flecked with stars. When the compass pointed to the correct course there was always one conspicuous star or a clump of them that I could line up with something in the rigging. Every now and then a glance at the compass would confirm that we were still on course. In the meantime I could immediately detect any tendency of the vessel to drift off course by looking at my chosen point. The captain was also checking some reference point of his own from wherever he was and could tell instantly when I did not hold her steady. He was not shy about letting me know my shortcomings. Our course that first night out of Bridgewater was easy to follow as it was due south. This took us well offshore and away from any hazards that lay near the land.

The day after sailing from Bridgewater the sky became overcast and the wind picked up. The captain, a very cautious man and well aware of his responsibility to bring the vessel, crew and cargo safely into port, must have felt comfortable with the topsails set, as they were not taken in. To my land-lubber senses we seemed to be making heavy going and I thought we might even have made better time if the topsails were doused.

I had not yet grown used to the sounds of the wind in the rigging. These sounds gave me the sensation of greater wind velocity than was probably true. The higher the velocity, the higher the pitch. We were at sea and there was no hill or other obstacle to cause the wind to veer or slow down. A wind from the southwest had hundreds of miles without obstruction; one from the southeast, thousands. The sound of the wind started as a low, gentle sighing, rather steady. The lowest pitch resembled "hhhhhh." As the wind picked up it began to put a "w" in front of the "h" as though it was puckering its lips. Soon it would add an "o" and would moan "whooooo," then "whaaaaa," then "whaaaay," then "wheeeee." As the force of the wind grew even stronger its voice would become a shriek that no letters can approximate.

Joining the sounds of wind in the rigging there were the creaks and complaints of the blocks as the motion of the ship increased and decreased the strain upon them. With no wind they rattled aimlessly in response to the vessel's slatting around in a ground swell. The jaws of the gaffs groaned against the masts and the masts themselves complained to the partners and steps that held them at the main deck and at the keelson.

Coming about was a noisy process. The boom tackles and sheet blocks rattled as the sails luffed and then squealed as we hauled on them to move the heavy booms over. The luffing canvas itself had different sounds depending upon the strength of the wind – a soft and muffled rumble when the wind was low, the beating of a rug over a clothesline when the wind was a little stronger, the pounding of a two-by-four against an empty board shack when the wind was strong enough to rip the tops off the waves. Then as the vessel heeled over and settled down onto her new tack the masts complained bitterly to their steps and partners until she settled into her new attitude. There was always noise of some kind or other on the run from Bridgewater to New York, as there was never a calm. Even the gentlest swell or slightest breeze kept the vessel creaking, a comfortable sound under those conditions.

For most of the ten days we were at sea on the run to New York we were on Georges Bank. This enormous expanse of the continental shelf extends from the Bay of Fundy nearly to Nantucket. For centuries it has produced an abundance of

Captain St. Clair Geldert (ca. 1879-1943) was the son of Captain and Mrs. George Geldert of Lunenburg, Nova Scotia. He shipped in local fishing vessels before becoming a merchant sailor and master. Among the schooners he commanded were the *John W. Miller, McLean Clan,* and *Jean F. Anderson.* For his merchant marine service during the First World War he received the Canadian Service Medal and Canada's Mercantile Marine Medal. He died of a heart attack at Yarmouth, Nova Scotia, in February 1943, as he prepared to take command of yet another schooner. (Photo by Knickle's Studio, Lunenburg, Nova Scotia)

Crew of the *Jean F. Anderson* at Newtown Creek, Brooklyn, New York. *From left*, Harry Nauss, Charles Turnbull, cook Ross Peeler, and Edmond Ellis — Frenchy. (Author's photo)

The author (right) and Mate Bill Snow at the *Anderson*'s rail. (Author's photo)

fish for Canadian and American fishermen. Then, in the 1960s and '70s, factory ships from Japan, the Soviet Union and other nations of Europe raided its wealth of edible protein. Petroleum geologists have prospected the formations under its bottom and have claimed the presence of oil. But none of this had developed in 1941. Then there were just some fishing boats and some freighters groping around in the fog without radar. There was probably an occasional German U-boat, but this was not the prime hunting territory for them. They preferred to prey along the shipping lanes where many troop transports and freighters loaded with goods zig-zagged toward England, North Africa and Russia. As the United States would not become a belligerent nation for yet another five months, German U-boat activity in the North Atlantic had not built up to its later effectiveness and terror.

We did not run as a vessel in wartime, as every night at sunset we lit and hung the red and green kerosene running lights. They gave out such a feeble glow, especially the green one in the starboard foremast shrouds, that I wondered how far they could be seen, even on a clear night. In the fog, when visibility was extremely poor, we sounded our foghorn. This was a rectangular box about two feet high by three feet long by one foot wide with a handle on the right side that turned a crank near the bottom. On the front there were two round holes, the large ends of twin horns. To operate the foghorn the lookout, the man on watch who was not at the wheel, would sit on this on top of the fo'c's'le and pump the crank vigorously back and forth. About five or six good pumps would give one decent blast on the horn. On the starboard tack we gave one loud toot about every minute. On the port tack we gave two toots instead of one. The sound the horn made was impressive and could be heard over a mile when the weather was clear and wind moderate. Fog is not ideal for the transmission of sounds. There is an uncertainty about it that always leaves a sailor wondering whether he has been heard. The acoustics of fog are treacherous. At times in fog a horn can be blasting its bellows out and not be heard more than two hundred yards away. At other times spoken words can be heard for over a mile.

One night on Georges Bank, in a dense fog and very little wind, we could hear a steamship. Because we could hear the rhythmic splash of a single propeller breaking the surface as well as the sound of the engine, we knew she was a small freighter running light with no cargo. We could hear an occasional clank, as though someone had dropped a wrench or a hatch toggle. We could hear the voice of a man as though coming through a pillow, muffled so that the words or even the language could not be identified. The steamer sounded no foghorn. At first her sounds seemed to be coming from more than one direction, but it soon became obvious that she was coming closer and we had no ability to get out of her way. We did our best, though. I pumped the foghorn crank as hard as I could, not waiting for the full minute to pass between toots. We were on the starboard tack. This technically gave us the right of way over all other vessels, but this legal technicality would do us little good if we were hit. Only a fool will stick up for his right of way at the risk of a collision. We all knew the age-old ditty of unknown authorship:

> "Here lies the body of Jonathan Day,
> Who died defending his right of way.
> Right, dead right, as he sailed along,
> Now he's as dead as if he'd been wrong."

In the meantime the captain had gone below and run back up with a flashlight in each hand. These he shone on the spanker so as to make the vessel more conspicuous. The steamer came right on and made no sign of changing course. She loomed out of the fog off our starboard bow, her course nearly parallel with, but opposite to ours. Her black shape rose high above our deck level, and her height and length made our hull seem frail and insignificant. As she thumped on by us we could see no light or human form. She was a silhouette except for the dim details of the pounding propeller and the white foam against the rudder. Nameless, nationless, apparently soulless, she evaporated back into the fog astern. I had forgotten that I was cold and miserable and that my feet were numb in their wet sneakers. We had had a near miss and we were all thankful still to be sailing "by the wind" toward Nantucket.

The incident of the freighter in the fog got me thinking about how helpless we were against another vessel, especially if her captain happened to be an enemy of the British and wanted to damage this barely significant fragment of His Majesty's merchant marine. We were totally unarmed, highly visible (except in fog), slow to move and stubborn to maneuver, and loaded with a cargo of some value to the Canadian economy and to the war effort. We weren't worth a torpedo that had been transported over three thousand miles in the limited space within a German submarine. The most cost-effective way to dispose of us would be either a shell from the deck gun, a couple of sticks of dynamite secured below the mainmast chainplates, or a bucket of our gasoline or their diesel oil and a match in the galley or beside the mainmast. The deck load of spruce would make a fine bonfire and we would have no possibility of putting it out.

In either case – fire or a round from the deck gun – we would have had to leave the vessel in the dory. We had no lifeboat as such and no life preservers, or even a life ring that could be thrown to a man in the water. The dory was a work boat with one pair of oars. It was used for painting and maintaining the topsides when in port and could be rowed ashore if the vessel were anchored or aground. It was not equipped with water, provisions, spare oars or a sail. Nevertheless it was all that was available and we would have been thankful for it if things got that bad.

We had another exciting encounter one bright, calm night on Georges Bank. A whale intercepted us and stayed with us for over half an hour. He lazily swam around the vessel. I imagine he was feeding on something and enjoying the companionship of our hull while doing so. As we had no engine or propeller noise and moved very slowly, he must have found us not unpleasant to be near.

While I was at the wheel he slowly came close enough to the starboard quarter so that Harry and I could see blotches on his back and see his blow-hole open and close. And, as he was to windward, we could smell his breath. It was warm and humid and smelled somewhat like low tide near a fishing wharf, but it had a muskiness, too, that was new to me. In what was either a gesture of friendship or amorousness, or merely a whim to scratch an itch, he rubbed his bulk four or five times against our quarter. I have no idea how large he was, as he showed only part of himself at any one time, but he was massive enough to send vibrations through our hull. I suspect that his contact with the rough wooden planking was not as pleasant as he had thought because afterwards he seemed to lose interest and wandered off into the night.

One Sunday the weather was fair enough to wash clothes. Sunday was the only day that we were allowed to do laundry and we took advantage of the break in the weather to do it. The same bucket that had so many other purposes we also used for a laundry tub. The cook kept a watchful eye on the amount of water we used, as our supply of fresh water was limited. We used cold water and our own cakes of soap. One rinse was allowed and then the clothes were tied in the standing rigging with yarns that had been raveled from a short length of old rope. This was before synthetic fabrics made drip-dry washing known to American and Canadian housewives. I was sure that wringing the clothes out as dry as possible would make them dry faster. I tried to prove my point by using my technique alongside Harry's dripping dungarees. They both dried in the same length of time.

One day, either from high spirits or from nervousness (I don't remember which), I began to whistle. It was no more than a silly little tune or portion of one, but it was enough to cause a commotion. The captain, who had been below shaving, dashed up his companionway, razor still in hand and face still half-lathered. With words that left no doubt and that frightened me with their unreasonable ferocity, he lashed into me. There was to be no whistling in this vessel, not as long as he was in command. He was so red in the face and was breathing so heavily that I would not have been surprised to see him burst a blood vessel. Actually I almost hoped that he would. Harry told me later that whistling in a vessel brings the worst kind of bad luck, usually in the form of a severe storm that does a lot of damage. This time no storm came, no unusual weather, no damage.

The man at the wheel was not allowed to smoke, although it was permitted at any other time and in any other place. I had no interest in smoking, but the idea of being forbidden to smoke at the wheel made me angry. After we got ashore in New York I bought a package of Beech-Nut chewing tobacco for the sole purpose of chewing it while at the wheel and spitting the sweet brown juice on the deck. My rebellion didn't last long because only the first taste of tobacco was pleasant and it made me crave water.

Although we were all together in close quarters, I never got to know my shipmates well. There was no conversation between us deckhands and the captain or the mate.

The captain, St. Clair Geldert, was from Lunenburg and had gone to sea all his life. He was sixty-two years old, and from my teenage vantage point he was ancient and rickety indeed, certainly older than my forty-five-year-old parents. He had poor vision and a thick Lunenburg German accent. I only saw him smile once.

The mate, Bill Snow, age fifty, came from Newfoundland – Brigus, I think. He smiled often and squinted all the time. I would have liked to know him better, but his natural uncommunicativeness combined with the protocol that separated officers and crew did not allow it. Ross Peeler, the cook, Harry Nauss, my watchmate, and Frenchy, the mate's watchmate, talked, but that was almost exclusively at mealtimes.

Harry was thirty-four and also came from Lunenburg. He had worked in various capacities ashore, mostly as a laborer, but he liked to go to sea frequently. He had been going to sea since he left school. I never found out how much schooling he had had, but he could read and he wrote a good letter. He had made many trips to the Caribbean and had worked in steamers

as well as sailing vessels. Although he missed the companionship of the opposite sex while at sea, and he was fond of
recounting his sexual exploits, he felt more at home when at
sea.

Frenchy, at forty-seven, was older than my father and
was a tough, scrawny little guy. He had the fierce look of a
falcon, which was intensified by a short beard of half grey and
half black, and a head of short hair that went in every direction
at once. His total lack of teeth made his beard jut forward in a
decisive manner. Frenchy's real name was Edmond Ellis, a fact
that he preferred to keep to himself. He came from Bridgewater
where he augmented his other income by bootlegging and doing odd jobs. Conversation was mainly between Harry, Frenchy
and Ross, with me as audience. Their topics included what the
vessel and the captain were doing and how well; the weather;
what they did when they were last ashore; what they would do
when they got ashore next; fornication (this was also included
in the last two topics); and other trips on other vessels. They
also savored stories of their rum-running adventures. They, as
well as nearly everybody else they knew who had been old
enough at that time, had been involved in rum-running. I was
envious because it seemed like the greatest game they had ever
played. This was the first trip any of us had made in the *Jean
F. Anderson* and, although no one realized it then, also the last.

New York: A Poor Relation Through the Front Door

During the ten days we were at sea on the way to New York the sun shone little. There were few days when the captain was able to get his noon latitude shot of the sun. Most of the time he had to navigate by dead reckoning. The taffrail log was paid out astern as we took our departure from West Ironbound Island. The captain read its dial frequently and went below to his charts. As we were beating most of the way and jibed or came about frequently, he must have drawn a complicated zig-zag course on the chart. From the time we sailed to the time we saw Sandy Hook at the entrance to New York Harbor we sighted no land either day or night. At no time were we able to see a lighthouse or even its flashing to help fix our position. I was amazed then, as I am now, that we came straight to *Ambrose* lightship. It is a testimony to Captain Geldert's years of dead reckoning experience and his intimate knowledge of the waters through which we passed. I suspect, too, that he was attuned to signals that I did not then consider or recognize.

The afternoon of the day before we sighted the lightship we became aware of the land. Long Island was still over the horizon, but it gave us ample evidence of its presence. The clouds above it didn't look like those ever seen over the ocean. The waves became shorter and more choppy as the sea became more shallow. The water changed and became greyer in color, and it had more bits of trash, things that people no longer wanted, floating in it. Most of all, we were aware of the smell of the water and the pollution that it carried out to sea. There were also smells from the land – thick fragrant odors of vegetation and raw earth. Most noticeable of all, however, were the smells of burning, of industrial fumes, and of garbage, the by-products of civilization that no one wants to be reminded of.

That night darkness never completely fell. The glow in the sky from millions of electric lights produced the effect of an eight hour dusk. Although no moon shone, we could see well enough to make out one another's features and to see a stray rope where it had fallen on the deck, even though they were both nearly the same color. Having grown up on the western fringe of that glow, I had never noticed it. But Georges Bank had conditioned me to nights that were illuminated only by nature. The contrast from a sky free from light pollution to the sudden arrival in its midst was dramatic. Since then I have never been unaware of any man-made glow in the sky. It destroys the beauty and magic of the night and it overwhelms and obscures all the wonders of astronomy except the planets, the moon and the brightest of the stars.

Ambrose lightship was unexpectedly awe-inspiring. Its bright red hull, high in the bow, was shaped not at all like one that was intended to move free from her anchorage. It was designed to ride at anchor through the worst possible hurricane winds and seas. She bucked at the end of her chain like a Brahma steer with an uncomfortable cinch and reared up high enough so we could see the curvature of her bottom up forward.

Harry explained to me that the men in a lightship were more bothered by seasickness than were men on any other kind of vessel.

The motion of the *Jean F. Anderson* in the same swell that tossed *Ambrose* seemed as nothing. Of course I had grown used to it, but the inertia of our cargo and the steadying force of the wind in our sails were calming influences and reduced the vessel's motion. If the wind had stopped, our motion would have increased considerably, especially the side-to-side roll. If, with no sails set, we had anchored near the *Ambrose*, our motion would have been similar to that of the lightship, but we would have fared worse because of our heavy load and because our hull was not designed specifically to ride at anchor. Our bow would have charged down into every trough and risen slowly carrying a load of solid water aft over the deck and deck load. In a storm the *Jean F. Anderson* would have torn herself apart and lost her deck cargo.

The *Ambrose* was designed to be a cross between a ship and a buoy. At night her light was meant to be seen by approaching ships and by day her red superstructure was appropriate for above-water visibility. She notified the harbor pilot vessel by radio of every ship that approached from the sea and could talk with any radio-equipped ship. We had no radio of any kind. The only electricity in the vessel was in the flashlight batteries and the dry cells that sparked the two one-lunger engines. Radar was only in the development stages, and none of the sophisticated electronic means of navigation had yet been perfected. Even so, by contrast with other seagoing vessels of that time, the *Jean F. Anderson* was an antique and was hopelessly inefficient.

Out of nowhere, it seemed, the pilot arrived and boarded us for the trip into the harbor. He was an agile, athletic man of probably thirty-eight. He leapt aboard like a chamois jumping to a new alpine perch. Immediately he made all of us aware that he was in complete command of running the vessel and that his passion was to put the schooner through her paces and to push her to her limit.

He had us set the topsails again and we headed in, leaving Sandy Hook on our port. The wind was coming straight down the harbor from the Battery and was steady and moderate. Harry, Frenchy and I had scarcely finished setting the three topsails when we were ordered to set "Josie's Coat," the fisherman staysail. This was the first and last time on the whole trip that we bothered with that sail. It was only meant to be used in steady light breezes and was positioned to capture and extract any help from the wind that might otherwise escape between the spanker, mainsail, main topsail and mizzen topsail. It, like all others of its kind, was a shabby quadrilateral sail made new from many pieces of old sails. There was no need for the cloth to be as rugged as the working sails, and new sailcloth would have been a waste of money. Josie's Coat, in reference to Joseph's coat of many colors, was an appropriate name as the whole sail resembled a crazy, disorganized quilt of varying shades of grey patches. We had a hard time setting it as none of us was familiar with what line went through which block and belayed where.

As the wind was coming straight down the harbor and we were going straight up it, our course was a beat to windward. Our conservative captain blanched at the way our pilot handled the vessel. He would wait until the very last minute before giving the order to come about. One time he came so close to a wharf on Staten Island that a softball tossed underhand from the wharf would have landed on our deck. The pilot, obviously enjoying himself, must have been happy not to have had the comparatively boring assignment of piloting a steamship from Sandy Hook to the Narrows. For him that would have been as exciting on such a fine day as driving a car to the store a mile away.

Before the command "Hard a-lee" was given we had to completely douse the fisherman staysail because it would have been in the way of the mainsail and main topsail. Then the fore and main topsails had to be clewed up. As there was a fair breeze with no sea running in the harbor, the main boom tackle was hooked up onto the main boom and was not in use. Then came "Hard a-lee" and the rest of the maneuver was performed as usual, except that the spanker boom was hauled to windward with its boom tackle as the sheet was eased so as to add torque and bring the vessel about more quickly. Finally the fisherman had to be reset. By the time all this was done we had but a few minutes to breathe and wipe off the sweat before going through the whole procedure again on the other side of the harbor. After several tacks the pilot must have realized that there was too little to gain through the use of Josie's Coat, so it was left in a heap on the deck. There was no time to fold and stow it then. He must have seen, too, that we were shorthanded and that his exuberant dash up the harbor was taxing to all hands. The cook was the only one not running around casting off lines and making others fast. A stranger would have thought the captain and the mate were just two more deckhands. They, too, were sweating and puffing from the exertion. The captain was also sweating for another reason: his ship was being handled in a manner he obviously considered imprudent.

Sweat or not, I enjoyed the run up to our anchorage in the quarantine area of the Narrows. It was fun to do our best, and exciting to see the vessel do her utmost. The pilot left us after we dropped anchor and all sails were down and in disar-

The *Jean F. Anderson* amid the industrial decay of Newtown Creek, Brooklyn. The fore gaff is hoisted to serve as a derrick for swinging out the lumber cargo. The schooner's white paint has already turned grey from the polluted atmosphere. (Author's photo)

ray. We had nothing furled when the customs and immigration officer came aboard from a motorboat. "And where is the American," I heard him say. He called me down into the cabin and questioned me about how I was being treated and what my plans were. I was embarrassed. The captain stood smiling benignly, supressing his nervousness by gripping his suspenders and rocking on his heels.

Harry, Frenchy and the cook were clearly displeased that I had withheld the truth of my actual residence and citizenship from them. "Why didn't you tell us the truth?" I squirmed, but they finally understood and they all accepted me back into their good graces. We knew that we had to rely on one another and that we were too small a group to tolerate any division among us.

That afternoon our tug arrived. Again I gave thanks for the forward donkey engine. It haltingly weighed the anchor. Link by link the chain came up and fell into the chain locker in the forepeak. But the tug was patient and eventually the muddy anchor was snug in the hawse-pipe. The captain took the wheel and the vessel meekly followed the tug. Our hawser was short, and the heavy black coal smoke from the steam-powered tug enveloped us and slowly dispersed astern. It angered me to see the soot-laden black billows soiling our sails. They had been washed by pure ocean rainwater, then bleached by the sun and salt spray to a lovely silvery sheen. Now as I watched they were being sullied by the foul breath of the machine age. I also resented our graceful vessel's demotion from an autonomous being, complete with its own soul and family, a world of its own, a proud and independent one, to a tethered captive led with a ring in her nose up past Governor's Island and into the East River. The farther we went the more oppressively civilization wrapped itself around us.

The buildings of lower Manhattan towered over us and made our tall masts look as trivial as those on a bathtub toy. Even the ferryboats and barges made our graceful hull look puny. But the ignominy of being the tug's captive was the worst aspect of that short trip. We – vessel, crew and cargo – seemed like a small, naughty child being dragged by a tyrannical teacher to the principal's office for discipline. As we went along we furled all sails except the foresail. It gave us something else to think about. Our course turned right from the East River into a foul open sewer called Newtown Creek. It divided Brooklyn from Queens and was dedicated to all that was hideous and vile-smelling.

Where we finally made our berth, Newtown Creek was no more than three times the width of our beam. We tied up on the left side at the Cross, Austin and Ireland lumberyard. Behind us was a coal barge. Ahead of us were decaying bulkheads and mounds of trash, possibly the rubble from a condemned tenement, everything salvagable having been removed. Across from us everything on land was black. The black bulkhead rose out of the black liquid in which we floated. Behind it piles of fine coal rose from a coal-surfaced yard. Black conveyors and cranes stood beyond the piles and beyond them were black gas tanks that supplied the gas stoves in that part of the city.

I now found out why the foresail had not been furled. Harry and I were told to unlace the head of it from the gaff and to swing the boom and sail outboard, away from the lumber yard. Then the longshoremen took over. We were not allowed to interfere. Only they could manage the unloading of the cargo. One of them ran our donkey engine, which was rigged up with a line through a block at the end of the foresail gaff. The other end of the line hung down to a sling that two other long-

High above a string of coal barges in Newtown Creek, the author stands at the tip of the *Anderson*'s jibboom. (Author's photo)

shoremen put around bundles of spruce furring. As the donkey engine lifted the load, the other men ashore hauled on a line fixed to the gaff and swung and guided the load into position on a waiting truck.

In the short time that our deckload had been exposed to the elements its original brightness had been tarnished with a greyish cast. Underneath the top layers, however, the color and freshness of the wood remained as it was when it left the sawmill.

Frenchy, Harry and I, our work area limited so as to keep out of the unloading activity, were put to work scraping paint. It wasn't long before I became aware of the worst feature of Newtown Creek. Bubbles rose to the surface between floating garbage and condoms from the waste that had been flushed down the toilets of Brooklyn and Queens. The condoms were referred to by everybody as "white eels." The bubbles, which accounted for most of the stench of the place, were mostly methane and hydrogen sulfide produced by the decomposition of fecal matter and sewage sludge that covered the creek bottom. In the winter, the longshoremen told us, mothers would bring their children with whooping cough to stand on the bridge about a hundred yards upstream from us. They were made to stand there for hours and inhale the fumes from the water. Such was the enlightened state of folk medicine in Brooklyn and Queens in 1941.

Not only was an atmosphere this high in methane and hydrogen sulfide unhealthy to breathe, it would have been lethal if the concentration were raised. We never heard of any fatalities caused by it in that area, but it was hydrogen sulfide that killed hundreds of people and thousands of animals when that same gas came from a geologic fault under a lake in Cameroon, West Africa, in 1986.

Looking aft from the jibboom. At left amidships, on the face of the long raised quarterdeck, near the stern of the dory stowed on the forward house, can be seen one of the small hatches for loading long timbers into the *Anderson*'s hold. (Author's photo)

Hydrogen sulfide gave us another problem that we would curse for several weeks. The sulphur from the gas reacted with the white lead in the vessel's paint to form lead sulfide, a black compound. During the days and nights we lay there the white paint gradually turned black.

One morning there was a commotion at the barge behind us. A man's body was being pulled out of the creek. It was the barge "captain." He had been out drinking at a neighborhood bar the night before and had lost his footing when boarding his barge afterwards. He, like most men of the sea at that time, could not swim.

Shortly after our arrival in Newtown Creek my father came to visit. He had come directly from his work in Manhattan and was dressed as a proper businessman should be. He looked out of place on the schooner and in that festering neighborhood. He was glad to see me, and I him. He let me take his "vest pocket" Kodak up the mast and out to the end of the jibboom to take pictures while he talked with the captain. Everyone felt awkward while he was there because he was from a different world, a world that none of the others had experienced or could ever become a part of. Frenchy told him that if he brought him a length of new sailcloth, he would make him a mantlepiece fringe. This he would do by raveling about a foot of the cloth, leaving only a few inches intact at the top. Then he would tack the cloth onto a board and combine the hanging threads with various patterns of square knots. Today we know the technique as macrame. Then it was purely an old-time sailor's pastime called "square knotting."

Saturday night came and I went home to East Orange, New Jersey. Everything seemed strange except the subway and the tube to Hoboken. I felt like a different person suddenly thrown back into surroundings that a month ago were seen through different eyes – the eyes of a nonworking American landlubber, college student, middle-class suburbanite.

My father made me strip on the back porch and get into a bathrobe. He had become well acquainted with the cooties (lice) and other crawling things that bedeviled the quality of life in trench warfare twenty-five years before. I had no bugs, but I went along with his request. A soak in the bathtub felt unusually luxurious and left a heavy black ring on the white glaze – so thick that it was hard to scrape and scrub off.

Waking up Sunday morning between clean sheets in a real bed in my spacious bedroom accentuated all the differences between my life and that of an old-fashioned ordinary seaman at sea on an obsolete windjammer. That Sunday at home in East Orange I reveled in the most ordinary things, things that I had accepted as commonplace or to which I had never given any thought at all. They took on an aura of luxury that I had never noticed. The flush of the toilet seemed as much of a treat as the napkin and the flat silver at the dining table. But the day was all too short, and soon I walked to the train station and rattled back over the rails to Greenpoint and my cramped bunk of boards and straw.

I found that hope, stimulation of the intellect, and an optimistic forward view remained ashore. A niggardly reward for endless drudgery was the compensation of a mariner, together with brief pauses to regain shore legs and to yarn about the romance of the seven seas. The mariner was never ashore long enough to reestablish wide-ranging shore ways; consequently his intellect rusted and his social skills atrophied. At sea he was subjected to exploitation, superstition, and to demeaning traditions and living conditions. He could afford only a bleak outlook for the future. Something else beyond what I had seen must have motivated John Masefield to write his infectious lyric praise of life at sea. My trip was not half over; I would have more time to seek the answer, more experiences before the mast.

A cat may have nine lives, but a sailor has three – all different: at home, at sea and tied up in port. Everything is different about being at home – the white sheets, the people, the food, the language. Each of these three lives demands different activities, routines and responses from the sailor.

I found a surprising difference in living pattern between being at sea and being tied up in port. As soon as we made the vessel fast to the shore, our routine changed. We now all worked the same schedule and, in this respect, resembled landsmen. Unlike landsmen, we could not return to our homes and families at night, my visit to East Orange being the exception. The fo'c's'le was nearby, safe and familiar – one of the benefits of this job.

One evening, like the longshoremen, we three deckhands walked to the nearest bar. The heat that day was severe and the humidity made it seem worse. A tall, cold glass of beer – just one – made everything seem worthwhile and put distance between us and the endless scraping of paint and the foul stench of the neighborhood. We all bought cheap cotton caps at a dimly-lit shop in the same block. Frenchy stopped me as I reached in the cap to pull out the roll of crumpled tissue paper around the edge. "Leave it in," he said. "It makes the cap look better longer."

The captain and the cook went off together soon after unloading had begun. They came back with provisions to last for a month. Jello was one of the new purchases they added to our diet. Rice was another.

As the original supply of flour had run out, the cook baked bread right away with the new American flour. Although he made it exactly the same as he always did, the bread turned out very differently. It tasted more like the bread I had been used to eating in the United States and not at all like that baked in Canada. We all preferred bread made from the Canadian flour, but we ate just as much of the new American kind, regardless. The cook was at a loss to explain why there was a difference. Years later I found out that Canadian flour is milled more finely than American flour. It is this fineness alone that accounts for the difference in results. Today, many Canadians who winter in Florida carry their flour south with them.

Ever since I had met Frenchy he had impressed me with his grizzled beard. It fitted his face so well and jutted out so fiercely from the point of his chin that it was his most striking feature. Without it he simply wouldn't be Frenchy. To my dismay, and over my protest, he shaved it all off the day after we tied up in New York. The pale wrinkled cheeks and sunken lips that had been hidden underneath looked weak and did not suit the sparks that still darted from beneath his dark, shaggy eyebrows. Not until the beard grew back did Frenchy again become Frenchy.

There was an element of envy in my regard for Frenchy's beard. Even at the advanced age of eighteen I was unable to produce much more than a little fuzz on my own chin. I was one of those blond kids who took agonizingly long to mature and even longer to need to shave regularly. From my vantage point forty-nine years later, this universal impatience to grow older seems the height of idiocy. Each stage of life gives its own cause for thankfulness. Each stage is too soon past and there is no returning.

Soon after unloading started the decks were free from their burden and the hatches could be opened. Slowly the vessel rose in the water and our sailing time approached. We were out of place. Here the vessel was lifeless and we were not free men, but were as birds with our wings clipped, prevented from our rightful function.

A feature unique to the *Jean F. Anderson* was the pair of small vertical hatches for loading extra-long timbers and spars from the main deck aft into the 'tween decks beneath the unusually long poop deck. These could now be seen.

Harry was given the job of cleaning out the water tank. He drained the remaining water and unbolted the manhole cover on the top. Once inside he chipped with hammer and blunt chisel until all the loose cement lay on the bottom. Suddenly there was not enough time to reline the tank with cement, so he hastily rinsed it out and filled it from the hose on shore.

As aggravating as it was to be towed behind the same smokey tug, all hands moved about with a new and livelier spring in our step as we cast off. There was no room in the creek to turn around, so the tug pulled us out backwards as far as a wide place. There we warped around into a less ignominious relationship with the tug. More importantly, being towed bow forward allowed us to steer. The wind was from the northwest, so there was no need to beat down the harbor from the Narrows where we took on the pilot and got sail on her. Good riddance, black smoke. Farewell, tug, yard engine of the harbor.

Light to the S'uth'ard

Leaving the harbor the pilot had no opportunity to play around with a borrowed schooner. With the northwest wind and all sails set and drawing, except Josie's Coat, it was a fast and easy reach down past Sandy Hook. There was no need to tack. The pilot turned over the wheel to the captain and then leapt lightly into the launch that had come alongside for him. It seemed like no time at all that we had cleared *Ambrose* lightship and were watching it grow smaller astern.

It was a relief to feel the vessel's deck rise and fall more slowly and rhythmically as the deeper water allowed the long ocean swells to stretch out and run freely. We breathed deeply of the clean air which we had missed so much in New York and watched the sea water regain its original clarity and brilliance.

Even before we said good-bye to the New York harbor pilot, I was put to work removing all traces of our stay in Newtown Creek. The captain was determined to make the vessel clean and bright-looking again. The sound paint that could not be scraped off became our target. We had to attack the white paint that had been blackened by hydrogen sulfide and coal dust and to make it white again. The captain, aware that drastic treatment was needed, mixed up a bucket of "soojee" by adding a half box of Oakite to one bucket of water. (The label recommended two teaspoonfuls to a bucket of water.) Using this caustic solution we scrubbed the paint with rags. The blackened paint yielded stubbornly and eventually became off-white. We had actually scrubbed and dissolved away the contaminated top layer. Quicker than that was the disintegration of our rags. When a rag was reduced to a handful of pulp we wrapped it in a fresh one.

After two days of soojeeing no rags were left in the vessel and our hands were in such bad condition that we could not open them fully without causing the cracks in our palms to bleed. With hands like this, hauling on ropes felt like hauling on fine barbed wire. Fortunately, the captain's supply of Oakite ran out and we had nothing else that could brighten the darkened paint. There was no alternative left but to break open the white lead paint and let our hands begin to heal while wielding a paint brush.

The *Jean F. Anderson* acted like a different vessel now. She no longer labored sluggishly under her heavy deck load, her bow digging deeply into each oncoming wave. No longer did we occasionally get our feet dunked when out at the end of the jibboom furling the flying jib. We were travelling "light," with only the inoperative diesel engines in the hold. Without cargo the vessel rode high in the water. Where before she rode the sea like a cormorant – low and wet – now she rode light and dry as does a herring gull. Coming about was easier now, so we stopped backing the forestaysail with the tailrope. Ideally, when a cargo is unloaded another is put aboard. That way the vessel is earning her keep on each leg of her voyage. Second best is to take ballast aboard. The added weight lowers the hull in the water and allows it to make less leeway (slip sideways less), thus making better time when the course is to windward. But, as ballast was uneconomical to load in New York, our holds and decks were empty. The ship's agent could find no southbound cargo for us. Sailing light may have cost us and the owner more dearly than we then realized.

The northwest wind held through the first afternoon, and we made enviable time through the water and over the bottom. It looked as though we would make a fast trip to Jacksonville, Florida, where the vessel was to pick up a load of hard (yellow) pine. Although I enjoyed the exhilaration of sailing fast in the right direction and not having to tack, I was concerned that the trip would end too quickly. Jacksonville would be the end of the trip for me; I had to sign off there. If I stayed with the vessel long enough to haul the pine to Bermuda, I would miss the start of the fall semester at Wesleyan. But I worried that if the passage was too short I might miss more seagoing experiences.

My concern was needless. The evening of the day we sailed the wind shifted to the south, and we began beating to windward again. The captain was probably fearful of running afoul of Cape Hatteras and its dreaded shifting shoals, final port of call for thousands of shipwrecks and the graveyard of many valiant men. He must have believed that the wind would blow from a more favorable direction farther out to sea, so he kept us beating a little to the east of south.

The third day after we left New York, the water suddenly changed and so did the sky. I had never seen water such an enchanting shade of intense blue. There was a distinct line of separation in the water between the cold-looking North Atlantic green and the blue Gulf Stream. We could see the change in the water about a mile away. The change in the sky was visible farther than that – maybe ten miles. If seen close to home, the clouds over the Gulf Stream would have signaled squally weather or rain. They were low and looked threatening. Harry assured me that they were normal for the Gulf Stream and did not mean trouble.

Harry and Frenchy told me of winter storms they had been in when the rigging became coated with ice and the vessels began to act top-heavy and were in danger of foundering. Ice would accumulate faster than it could be chopped away. If they were within reach of the Gulf Stream, they would run for it. Once within its embrace, the warmth would melt the ice effortlessly. They only had to be on the lookout for chunks of it falling on them from aloft. In this way the friendly Gulf Stream saved many a vessel, many lives, and many hours of hard labor.

It was exciting to be in the Gulf Stream, this river without banks that flows from the tropics diagonally across the North Atlantic. It prevents the British Isles from having a climate like that of Labrador, which is on the same latitude. Instead, it allows palm trees to grow in Cornwall and bathes the islands in abundant rainfall, keeps the Emerald Isle eternally green and English gardens smiling. It also brings fog to Nova Scotia, Newfoundland and the Grand Banks as well as nourishment to untold millions of fish on the banks.

In the water floated many mats of a type of yellow seaweed that was new to me. It was gulf weed or sargasso weed and came from that mysterious area of the ocean south of Bermuda. Frenchy, Harry and Ross told me stories about vessels that had been lost in that area – trapped in masses of this weed as large as counties and becalmed in regions where wind never blows above a whisper, and then only for minutes. The Sargasso Sea lies within the larger area that later came to be known as the "Bermuda Triangle." No doubt the lore and mystery of the Sargasso inspired much of the mythology of the Triangle.

One unexplainable, but undeniable, fact remains about the Sargasso Sea. It is the breeding ground for European and North American eels. Elvers (baby eels) born there return to the continent from which their parents came, but in their watery nursery they mingle indiscriminately.

Not long after we had entered the Gulf Stream my shipmates began to see and talk about flying fish. I couldn't see them and this bothered me. As hard as I strained my eyes they remained invisible to me. For a while I thought the men were kidding me and trying to get me to say that I saw them too, so they could have the fun of laughing and telling me that there was none to be seen and that I had an overactive imagination. The gullibility of the greenhand was always a legitimate source of fun at sea.

I was in a quandary for nearly two days and was annoyed that I could neither see a single flying fish nor uncover my shipmates' conspiracy – only one of which could have been possible. Then I took my trick at the wheel, with a brisk breeze blowing and the sun dazzling in a cloudless blue sky. This was true "flying fish weather." No other kind could make a sailor happier. I was not thinking about anything in particular, but was alert enough to be meticulously on course. Suddenly I saw a flying fish shoot out of a wave just below its crest. It was larger than I had expected and radiant with the lightest of rainbow colors. Its trajectory took it in a rather flat arc over fifty feet. I was both stunned and delighted. Suddenly there were flying fish everywhere – dozens and dozens. Their grace and beauty remain a part of my soul today and will never dim in memory. Neither will I forget my blindness to them that persisted for so long.

Maybe I was looking for something as small as a sardine that would flip out of water for only a second and fall back within a few feet. I don't know, but I was reminded of a story I had read about a shipwrecked Swedish sailor who was picked up by a pearl fishing boat in the South Pacific. The pearl fishermen had just lost their diver and none in their boat was willing or able to go down. The Swede offered to try it. With no one down there to show him what an oyster looked like on the bottom, he could see no pearl oysters in the strange world below. The whole crew was convinced they were there and kept urging the Swede to keep going down and looking. After hours of this exercise he suddenly saw one. As soon as he saw that one he recognized hundreds all around him. Twenty-twenty vision is not all that is necessary to see; I found out as he did. Seeing requires observing, knowing what to look for and how to look for it, a process that involves the mind more than just the eyes.

Ross told me that at night flying fish would often come aboard a vessel that was heavily laden and had her decks low to the water. In the morning the crew on watch would pick them up for the cook to fry for lunch. I never had that treat as our decks were too far above the water. He told me also that many natives of the Caribbean ate flying fish raw after they had been soaked a short time in lime juice.

Because conversation with the captain was taboo, we never knew the ship's exact position. But we in the crew performed our own imprecise brand of dead reckoning. Even without a chart or sextant, and not knowing what our net day's run was, we had a rough idea of where we were. We understood that the Gulf Stream was pushing us the wrong way – away from our destination as long as we were in it, but

The helmsman's view of the *Jean F. Anderson,* looking forward from the port quarter. The wheel is out of the picture at right. The companionway leads into the captain's quarters in the after house. (Author's photo)

we did not know how fast it was doing so. Why we remained in that magic river for so long we didn't understand. It must have cost us at least a hundred miles, because we stayed in it many days.

One afternoon two strange things happened. They both had to do with the land. We reckoned we were not far off Cape Hatteras. That the water was not deep was confirmed by the shortness of the seas. The water also took on a slightly cloudy look that we thought must be suspended silt or fine sand that had been stirred up by surf on the low-lying banks of North Carolina. Although there was not a glimpse of land, we could almost feel its presence over the horizon.

The first gift from the land was mine alone. It was poison ivy. I have always been susceptible to the vile stuff and I am certain that it was nothing else. It was a very light case and ran through its normal course. I can only conjecture that I got it from contact with something that I had previously worn in the woods and had not let rub against my skin until that time, or that it was airborne. Someone ashore might have had a brush fire with the noxious weed in it. Although none of us smelled smoke, the hot breeze was from the west and brought faint whiffs of raw earth and pine woods.

The second gift from the land affected all of us and was more disagreeable. It was a cloud of biting flies – thousands of them. They looked like ordinary house-flies, but the tip of the proboscis was sharp instead of the familiar blunt suction cup. They bit hard and from all sides. The captain armed himself with a flyswatter and smashed flies all over the inside of the cabin. Through the tightly closed windows we could hear him cursing them individually and as a species. The cook came forward and reported to us that the "old man" was swatting the same flies over and over again. Even with his thick glasses his vision was so poor that he couldn't distinguish between the live ones and the dead. After about two hours of torment the flies gradually left us – blown farther out to sea, there to bother no one and eventually to be eaten by living things of the ocean, another link in the interminable food chain that connects all life on earth. Long after the flies had left the vessel, the captain could be heard cursing and swatting the same dried-out, black corpses. Some of them were still on the wall two weeks later when I had to venture into those sacred premises.

After the flies, we headed out to sea and crossed the Gulf Stream again. This time we kept going to the east. The winds were constantly changing, but mostly they were too light to be of much help. Eventually, about eight days out of New York, Frenchy and Harry figured we must be almost to Bermuda. They must have had charts and instruments inside their heads. I did not. Then we headed south again and entered a region that favored us with squalls – several of them each day. We could see them in the distance and could anticipate their arrival well enough to have the topsails and jibs off, so we only had to contend with the larger sails when they struck. The dousing sequence was first the three topsails, then the jibs, starting with the outermost: the flying jib, the outer jib and the inner jib. Then the gigantic spanker would come down, then the foresail. Usually we rode out the squalls under forestaysail and mainsail. If the blow got too heavy, the forestaysail was the last to come down.

When danger from a squall was apparent, all hands, including the cook, turned out and raced furiously to avoid any mishap. Ross Peeler was not only a good and conscientious cook, he was faster and more nimble than any of us when it came to taking in sails at the start of a hard blow. He had the knack of always appearing at the most advantageous place at the right time. He could tame a walloping sail in less time and with less apparent effort than anyone else.

The principal part of taking in the jibs was letting go their halyards. That act and the casting off of the sheets relieved the force of the wind, but any wet canvas left banging around in the wind was difficult to approach and subdue. It was better that someone else cast off the halyards and sheets, one at a time, after you had crawled out to the far end of the jibboom. Then they would pull down the peak of the sail with the downhaul and you would tie the whole sail to the jibboom with the gaskets that were attached along both sides of it.

This was an easier and safer operation than furling the topsails, but it had risks and thrills of its own. There was none of the jerky, circular, whipping motion that you felt aloft. Instead, it was like riding on an elevator with a megalomaniac at the controls. One second you would feel yourself being shot high into the air; the next in a free-fall that ended with straining knees and sagging cheeks and feet buried in the foaming brine.

To protect men working on the jibs, American sailing vessels have netting strung beneath the bowsprit and jibboom. We had no such contraption, and the looks of the bow were not spoiled by it. I never felt anything other than exhilaration while taking in the jibs.

All the standing rigging of the *Jean F. Anderson* was galvanized wire tightened by turnbuckles. The days of dead-eyes and tarred rigging had passed before 1919, four years before I was born and the year that the schooner was launched in Port Wade, Nova Scotia. The running rigging (all the ropes that had to be manipulated to run the vessel, hoist and trim the sails, and move the booms) was made of sisal. Sisal rope was covered with short, stiff fibers that stuck out straight. To tender hands it felt prickly. To raw hands it was torture. To our normal, work-toughened hands sisal rope was easy to use and comfortable, and the fibers that stuck out made the line less likely to slip through our hands. Manila hemp – stronger, smoother, more supple and rot resistant – came from the tropical abaca plant and was too expensive to be used by a penny-pinching schooner owner. Real hemp rope, the forerunner of Manila hemp, is now unobtainable as it comes from the same plant that yields a more valuable crop: marijuana and hashish. It was the best rope available until Manila hemp came into use. Toward the end of the eighteenth century the British government ordered the Loyalist settlers in New Brunswick to plant many acres of hemp for the benefit of the Royal Navy and for the economic profit of the new settlement. In 1941 nylon and all the synthetic fibers had yet to be made commercially available in the form of cordage.

The mate was sympathetic with us when our hands were tender and bleeding, but we all knew we could not be excused from handling ropes. Haul we must. When we had hauling to do during the day he would encourage us with his standard doggerel:

"Up hands and down asses,

Makes stout lads for fine lasses."

The captain might join in with his, "All right, boys. Come a daisy onto it now." The mate's words had a rhythm that helped coordinate our efforts, but the captain's always fell flat.

The constant handling of sisal rope had toughened our hands quickly. Except for the time we were using Oakite soojee and recovering from it, we could do amazing things barehanded. Our hands were too calloused to be bothered by splinters. Frenchy bragged that he could pound a nail into a pine board with his palm, but I didn't believe him. When on watch one night, alone on the forepeak, I tried it myself. I was astonished that I could drive a ten penny nail far enough into a piece of white pine with one swat of my right palm to require a good tug to get it out. It didn't hurt, but I never did it again.

Ten days after leaving New York we used up the last of our white paint. It covered everything that needed covering and from the deck and from aloft the vessel looked pretty good. We had had so many good hard rain squalls that the soot from the tug and the city's atmosphere had all been washed out of the sails.

We were now somewhere south of Bermuda and between its longitude and that of the Gulf Stream. This region (around 30 degrees north latitude), known for sudden squalls and baffling light winds that punctuate flat calms, is referred to as the "horse latitudes." We seemed unable to get out of it and could make no apparent progress. We needed to keep an alert eye out in all directions, both for signs of danger and for indictions of some favorable gift of wind that we might profit by. As a result we were constantly making adjustments to our course and to the set of the sails. If it weren't for the need to run the vessel, and we had been ashore on some coconut-and-hibiscus island, this weather would have been no problem. There would have been ample rain and sunshine to produce a paradise. But we had to bring our vessel to Jacksonville in the best possible time. It was infuriating to work so hard and yet know we were going nowhere. The captain kept scratching his head and changing the course, and we kept pulling ropes and turning the wheel – all to no avail.

When we were truly becalmed and the water had become oily looking and flat, we could see objects floating on the water at a great distance. Sometimes we would drift right to the object, or it to us. It almost seemed that, if we stared long enough at a speck, it would become larger and eventually end up alongside. Mostly there were bits of driftwood, broken boards, logs, stumps, broken crates. There were one or two bottles, but we never got close enough to see whether they contained notes. There were no plastic things floating out there then, for this was before the era of the ubiquitous plastic packaging that Thor Heyerdahl reported seeing in the remotest areas of the ocean on his transatlantic papyrus raft trip in 1970.

One bright moonlit night we saw a speck directly in the path of the moon. We watched it for three hours as it came alongside, remaining clearly visible all the time. It was a coconut. Harry dipped it up in the faithful multipurpose bucket. We took turns shaking it and were awed by the sound of liquid inside. Surely it must be salt water. The next day the cook opened it and found that the milk was fresh and sweet. It contained no taint of salt water, although it had traveled hundreds of miles and might have been in the water for months. I could only feel reverence for the drive to survive and reproduce that manifested itself in that coconut. It took no imagination to understand how the tiniest atoll and the newest barrier island, no matter how remote, became a place of growing green things. With this thought in mind, that bit of coconut tasted sweeter than the daintiest chocolate truffle produced by man.

Frenchy, Harry, the cook and I had been talking about ambergris. Harry had known a sailor who had found some. It would have brought the man a lot of money if the captain had not confiscated it and sold it for the account of the vessel's owners. Just think of the vastness of the ocean and what the chances are of finding a deviant lump of whale scat floating about among the waves. Most of the time it is hard enough to spot a man in the water because of the size of the waves. Something the size of an orange, and not projecting above the surface, would be somewhere between impossible and extremely unlikely to find.

It wasn't more than hours after the ambergris conversation that Harry spied something shapeless drifting a hundred yards off the starboard bow. With agonizing slowness it drifted closer until it was within reach of the bucket. It was a gelatinous mass over two feet across. As it floated it wobbled and its shape undulated. It was not a jellyfish, but its color was like that of the white, transparent ones that wash ashore by the thousands in August along the beaches of the Maritimes. Harry and I both tried to dip the thing up, but it wouldn't oblige by staying in the bucket. Finally I pulled the bucket in and found that a piece of the thing had been torn off by the broken rim and was still in the bucket. It was obvious that it was not ambergris. Although none of us had ever seen ambergris, we all knew it had a strong, disgusting smell. Looking closely I could see specks spaced at regular intervals within the jelly mass. It looked so much like the frog spawn I had seen many times in ponds that I was sure it was the spawn of something large. Fortunately none of us had had a chance to spend the profits we had imagined almost within our grasp.

Within hours of reaching the Gulf Stream I had observed fish swimming and playing just ahead of the vessel. They seemed especially attracted to the leading edge of the stem and the bow wave as it curled outward and fell. These were dolphins, Harry told me, a joy to watch. They seemed to exist just for the enjoyment of their play and the companionship of our vessel's bow. They seemed in constant danger of being run over or being speared by the dolphin striker, which, of course, is the reason for the name of that short spar extending downward from the outer end of the bowsprit.

One Sunday I tried my hand at catching a dolphin. The cook obliged by giving me a scrap of salt pork for bait. In no time I hooked one. He came up thrashing and dazzled me with his magnificent colors. Seen from above he looked blackish and slender. The side view, which was visible as soon as the hook bit him, was broad and the color graduated from inky blue on the back through lighter blue and green to sunshine yellow beneath. I was not prepared for the intensity of the colors, nor was I expecting the rapidity with which they faded only minutes later as he gasped his last on the deck. Although the flesh was delicious and we all ate it with equal gusto, I felt true remorse for having taken the life of a creature so beautiful, so playful, so companionable. I will never harm another dolphin.

Moonstruck

"Don't," said Harry. Like an ideal older brother, he was always ready with considerate and usually helpful advice. "Don't let the moon get onto you when you're asleep. It'll take and draw you."

"That's right," said Frenchy. "I seen people that was drawn up so bad they couldn't get their hands more'n this far from their shoulders." He held his hands about ten inches apart to demonstrate the devastating power of the moon.

"I know a man what couldn't stand up like you 'n' me," said Harry. He bent over from his hips about 45 degrees from the horizon as proof.

Here it was Sunday night, the only day of the week when we were allowed to be on deck without working. It was stiffling hot and we were becalmed east of the Gulf Stream and south of Cape Hatteras. We hadn't seen land since clearing New York Harbor twelve days before. Our exact position didn't bother me much although I felt sure that even the captain didn't know it. He hadn't taken his noon sight with the sextant for several days because of noontime overcast – not typical for that part of the North Atlantic in early August. I didn't realize until later that I was right and the only use of the sextant that he knew was how to shoot the sun at its exact zenith. That, at least, gave him a fairly good fix for latitude.

No air moved inside the fo'c's'le and what air there was was steamy. The common-sense solution seemed to me to drag my straw tick out on deck and sleep there. Better yet, was to throw it down through the open forward hatch and sleep in the cooler depths of the empty hold. The sky was filled with stars that were larger than any real ones could be. The moon was just rising, and the whole scene seemed like pure John Masefield to me. Why would anybody want to sleep in his bunk on such a night?

Sometimes the guidance and clarity of common sense can fade in the face of a stronger appeal. This was one of those times. The obvious sincerity of my shipmates and the strange setting – a setting still connected in my mind more with fiction than reality – must have thrown me off. A fog bank of super-stition and mystery seemed to roll in from the Sargasso Sea and blot out the training of my intellect and the objectivity of my upbringing. In spite of the heat there came a slight prickling sensation and a chill at the nape of my neck as each hair root quickened.

They could be right. Were they not my shipmates and did we not help and look out for one another? In truth each of us, again and again, entrusted his life and safety to the hands and judgment of the other. We had to. Even if they were wrong this one time, they had seen much more of the world than I had and they had lived longer and had survived more dangerous predicaments than I probably ever would. They both had seen examples of the crippling results of sleeping in the light of the moon – actually seen them. If anybody knew, they must. Even if they were wrong, why should I take a chance? Somehow I managed to sleep in my own bunk that night. The heat was there, but at least the moon wasn't able to get to me.

Superstition dies hard, even in densely populated areas. Notice how often a sneeze causes a stranger to say, "God bless you," and see how few people dare walk under a ladder. Maybe Nova Scotia's intimate relationship with the sea, and the unaccountable events that her sons have experienced on lonely watches in the fog and at night, strengthens superstition's hold here. But it lingers on, even among those who have never been to sea.

Years after my close encounter with the moon – thirty-five years to be exact – I was telling my friend Cecil about this experience. He had seen a lot of the world himself and had lived in foreign lands. He had been in the army and could relate to this kind of story.

"Yes, I heard tell of things like that," he told me. "Sometimes a feller don't know just what to do when everybody else says something and they all agree. I know one old man told me he got drawn by the moon and he was never the same afterwards. His face was kinda drawn funny on one side and that side of his mouth didn't work right. He said the moon done it and he's a good church-going man, he was. Dead now, though."

"There sure are a lot of superstitious people around this part of the country," I said. "You don't believe that kind of thing, though. Do you?"

"Now don't go gettin' me wrong. You 'n' me know better 'n that. We seen enough of the world to know what is and what isn't. Matter of fact I slept in the moonlight once. Had to, and it didn't do nothin'. See?" He stood at attention and held both arms out straight toward me. They were well-formed and muscular and surely didn't look drawn. His whole appearance spoke of honesty and capability, the product of hard work and clean living.

I went on: "This moon superstition is something I've heard of only here in Nova Scotia. Don't you think it's one of those stories that sailors bring back from the tropics just to keep the landlubbers in their place?"

"Well, I don't know. I know I don't believe it and none of them other superstitions neither. People can sit around and tell you all kinds of things that just ain't so. It's all talk. I don't believe in none of them."

Then he looked at me straight on and with eyes wide open and absolutely sincere. "Of course, I do believe in fore-runners."

Jolted by this sudden turn in our conversation I asked the natural question. "What's a forerunner?"

"They's people what died and hang around. It's like they wasn't sorted out yet and don't know where to go."

"Come on, Cecil. You're not serious. You don't ..."

"I sure do." He looked just a trifle hurt. "I seen one once. In my father's house it was – at the top of the stairs. It didn't make no noise. It just walked right through the door. Door wasn't even open."

The Vessel's True Master

It seemed that we were stuck in the horse latitudes forever and it would be our fate to have the vessel rot out from under our decayed corpses, the entire ship's company having died months earlier from lack of water. The various pieces of the hull and rigging would then float in the same location for the rest of time or until they became waterlogged and sank. From that time onward our ghosts would remain on the surface, perhaps in some disguise, to haunt all hapless seafarers who drifted in. Perhaps our prolonged stay was arranged by some other miserable crew who had met that fate right there in the hazy past. Is there a single voice that would dare disagree? It is easy to scoff at such an idea from the land, but at sea the mind accepts possibilities even more bizarre than this.

All told, we were there for a full week, which of course, included one Sunday with its opportunity to enjoy the freedom of the deck while off watch. What could be better than a swim in this placid, warm water? Everyone except the captain was on deck and was horrified when I took off my clothes and climbed onto the rail. None of them would consider doing such a thing. Besides being modest and not wanting to expose their naked bodies to view, none except Ross could swim one stroke. This makes sense and is understandable as long as they were brought up where the water was perpetually cold, but not here where the water temperature was close to 80 degrees and the air hot and motionless. Ross, however, had lived in Florida for several years. He and all his family were good swimmers. Surely there could be no greater pleasure at this moment than to plunge head-first into this over-sized, solar-heated pool. Ross merely said, "I don't think I would do that."

Having waved at the spectators, I turned to dive. What I saw below nearly made me lose my balance. It certainly caused me to cancel my swim and any other swims I might have the opportunity to take voluntarily for the rest of the trip. There below me was the motionless form of the largest shark I could imagine. It could have swallowed me whole, Jonah-style. Its every detail was clearly visible over its entire twenty-foot length. It was just hovering there close to the surface in the shadow of the hull on the port side. Its dorsal fin protruded through the surface, but left no ripple. The fibers of the fin and texture of the skin were plainly visible as though through a magnifying glass. Two or three remoras were fastened with their suction cups behind the shark's gills. Half a dozen fish of about the same size swam lazily and nonchalantly all around the monster paying no heed to the danger of those dreadful teeth, sometimes only inches away. These were pilot fish and are commonly seen in the company of sharks. If fish are known by the company they keep, as people are, I give pilot fish the lowest possible rating.

To my surprise, no one laughed or teased me when I jumped back down to the safety of the deck. They all came and stared at the creature with more shaking of heads than of tongues. They had more than one reason not to go swimming.

The captain was furious when he heard of my intended swim. He forbade any further attempt to swim – not from his vessel or anywhere, not until I was discharged. I learned from my shipmate instructors that as long as the dolphins play around the bow there are no sharks close by. I didn't feel confident enough about this bit of sailors' lore to trust it – then or ever – even with the captain's blessing and with the most conscientious lookout standing by with an elephant gun.

From the safety of the deck I whiled away the rest of that afternoon fishing up bits of sargasso weed with the bucket and admiring its passengers. There were several very small fish that looked too delicate to survive in so dangerous an element as the sea. Best of all were the sea horses, which clung to strands of weed by curling their tails around them. They had a charm all their own that could almost be called a personality. They were certainly the most winsome creatures that the sea had shown me.

A stay in the horse latitudes must have depressed every crew of every wind-powered vessel that involuntarily sojourned there. In a short time every effort began to seem futile and one day merged with another like puddles of glue. Imagination quickly began to see an eternity of drifting among the sargasso weed and being tantalized by meaningless squalls. Without doubt Coleridge's *Rime of the Ancient Mariner* put into print what every hapless sailor felt when trapped there. Would it ever end? Could there really be trade winds anywhere? Are dry land and fair breezes only myths?

After a week in the horse-latitude prison the wind picked up and blew fair and strong out of the south. At the same time a heavy, low overcast moved in. With it came a bird that had such grace and yet such foreboding about it that I was charmed. Its body appeared small and suspended between its

long, thin wings. It was grey all over and seemed to fly effortlessly and without stressing its wings. It kept swooping as
though hunting for something it had lost and would never find.
It was larger than any gull. It made no sound, and yet it appeared to be mourning. It would skim close to the surface of
the water in a serpentine course and then rise above the height
of the topmasts without a flutter. It was an albatross. Of course,
Harry saw the grey visitor too, as we were always on watch
together. He was so disturbed by the bird that he could talk of
nothing else when we went off watch. He told us all, "By the
sweet, sufferin', dyin', all blue Jesus it had a bad look onto it.
Them fellers is always bad, but this one's got a livin' gale or
worse in his feathers."

Then there was an exchange of stories about how some
kind of disaster always follows the sighting of an albatross.
Frenchy added the voice of enlightenment. "Some of them old
timers," he said, "thinks they's sailors what got lost at sea in
bad storms and they been sent to warn other sailors they's a
bad blow comin'. They was a superstitious lot."

Superstitious or not, the tireless flight of the giant albatross hundreds of miles at sea is an awe-inspiring sight. The
albatross was extremely rare in these waters. There is no bird
about which man knows less, as they almost never are seen
close to land except to nest on a few deserted islands far from
shipping lanes or human habitation.

Strangely, the albatross with its ten-foot wingspan is a
close relative of the eight-inch-long petrels. These little birds
joined us as soon as the shore of Nova Scotia dropped below
the horizon. My shipmates called them "careys," but more
often they are called "Mother Carey's Chickens" or storm petrels. They were with us off and on most of the way to New
York. The name storm petrel indicates the belief that they are

seen just before a storm. Nobody knows who Mother Carey was or why these birds should be called her chickens.

The "careys" were a marvel to watch. They flew up and down the waves, so close to the water I couldn't understand how they could keep from frequent dunkings. They seemed almost to run up and down on the water and never flew more than a few yards on any fixed course. Night or day made no difference to them. They kept up their busy pace whether dark or light, rain or fair, emitting tiny high-pitched peeps all the while. I became attached to these tireless wanderers and actually felt sorry that they were destined by heredity to lead such a restless life without shelter or repose. They were company of sorts during the lonely night watches on the cold part of the trip.

Within hours of our sighting the albatross, the wind picked up and we were making good time through the water. Just as the sun was setting there suddenly appeared, coming in the opposite direction and passing the vessel no more than sixty feet to starboard, a whole herd of dolphins – the mammals, not the fish. To me they looked like porpoises, their cousins that are seen up north. It is confusing that this mammal is also known as a dolphin, but it bears no resemblance to the fish. Thanks to television (and "Flipper") and to modern aquariums, the mammal is now better known than the fish. Both have traits that endear them to man so much that they outweigh the animals' economic value. Both are uplifting to the spirits in a world that is too full of misery and ugliness. Both are friends of the sailor and keep him company far from land.

We had seen dolphins (the mammals) playing around the vessel several times before, but they were always alone or in pairs. They were always swimming lazily and appeared solely interested in sociability and leisure. At night we had seen them

swimming alongside, their markings and graceful shapes out-
lined with phosphorescent "devil's fire" and leaving luminous
trails behind them – our own personal comets.

The dolphin herd, however, was united in one purpose –
that of traveling as fast as it could and in a straight line. There
must have been thirty or forty of them. They were rushing
nearly downwind and their silver and black bodies shot completely out of the waves near the crests. They were bunched so
close together and they were out of the water so much of the
time that they appeared to be playing a crazy kind of leap-frog
while running a marathon. They moved so quickly that they
were past us and out of sight astern in less than a minute. The
captain was visibly disturbed, but said nothing. Dolphins
traveling fast and all together like that are a sign of a storm
approaching. We deckhands did not know what the captain's
barometer was telling him.

As the light faded from the sky, the wind died and the
vessel was left to wallow miserably with her sails and rigging
slatting around noisily. Lightning began in the distance and
made rapidly toward us. We immediately began to take in sail
as fast as possible. When the squall was nearly upon us the
captain called the cook up to help take in the spanker and
foresail. As the foresail was being lowered the squall hit with
such force that it knocked the schooner way over and the
foresail became as hard to grab as a team of stampeding horses.
The heavy wet canvas seemed to explode with loud bangs and
defied any grip that we might take on it. Slowly, and with five
of us struggling with it, we subdued the beast with several
lines. Then came the mainsail. That was worse. Finally we
were riding before the storm under forestaysail alone and
making heavy going of it. The helmsman's job became nearly
superfluous. The vessel ran nearly before the wind, any other

course being impossible to steer. The whole time we were able to see clearly because of the nearly steady discharge of lightning.

The wind was screaming with a high pitch and so loudly that human voices became useless. Harry was on lookout up forward. I was at the wheel and the captain was twenty feet away at the starboard quarter. I was nearly blinded by the lightning because it was so close and so constant. It hit our mastheads numerous times and ran down the rigging. It arced from the chainplates to the water below them. One bolt must have passed between the captain and me, although neither of us could be sure what happened. He was knocked against the rail and I against the wheel. The brilliance and force of the explosion left us blinded for several minutes and our ears ringing and muffled for hours. I don't know why the lightning was not attracted to the metal in the wheel I was holding. Surely, if the captain were any taller, he would have been knocked right overboard. There would have been no possible way to reach him in that sea. We had no control over the vessel, and the storm had piled up the water into waves nearly fifty feet high and over two hundred feet from crest to crest.

All other squalls that we encountered were of short duration. Any thunderstorm ashore I have ever experienced hit a climax and then began to recede. Not this killer storm. We were in what seemed like the center of it for a full half hour. Then it left suddenly and all hands just held on tight and braced themselves because the helpless vessel, left without a breath of wind, could only roll violently. There was no need to set sails.

With the dawn came a light breeze, and the vessel steadied down as we got sail on her. The large yellow wooden balls that had decorated each masthead were gone; fragments of them were found on the deck. There was a scorch mark below one of the chainplates. Otherwise, there was no damage or injury. That we were spared seemed miraculous. We had been in the grips of the true master of the vessel and he had given us a good shaking. We all looked at one another and at our vessel with greater appreciation. Breakfast tasted better than ever.

Our big storm was the turning point in the weather. The breeze grew gradually all the next day, and by evening it was fresh and steady. We grinned at each other and shook our heads in disbelief – it seemed too good to be true. The clutches of the doldrums had been released. We could breathe deeply and feel free again. For three days we enjoyed a fair breeze and did not have to beat tediously to windward.

The captain then had us get the deep-sea (pronounced DIP-sea) lead line up from the lazaret. We hove to long enough to get our way off and threw the heavy lead weight as far forward as possible. It seemed to go down forever before it fetched up on the bottom. We were no longer riding over the abyss of the ocean, but had arrived over the continental shelf. That the lead could reach the bottom at all was proof of this, but the water had not become shoal enough to shorten the waves. Because the charts show a steady, gradual shallowing of the water as land is approached, and as the captain was able to get the vessel's latitude from his noon shot of the sun, he could fix our position closely and plot an exact course for the mouth of the St. Johns River. The latitude line intersected at nearly a right angle the line drawn between the soundings shown by the deep-sea lead line. Where the lines crossed was our position. We fell off the wind as we hauled in the lead line. Harry and I, working as fast as we could, were not able to get it all wound back on the reel before we had picked up way and were on our new course.

We made no comments about our course and the antici-
pation of a landfall. We all knew that we were getting close. It
was about time. Three weeks to travel from New York to
Jacksonville was about three times as long as expected. We had
used up all the water in the 500-gallon steel tank. We were
actually looking forward to this event because, without the
protection of the cement lining, the water had become rusty,
and it stung our gums and had a sharp, repulsive taste. The
water in the oak casks was no joy to drink either. It was slimy,
and it took an effort to swallow it. But we were not about to
run out of water, as there were two full casks remaining.

For one whole day we approached the Florida coast. Very
slowly the waves shortened, signifying the diminishing depth
of water. The seawater gradually became turbid, and we saw
clouds ahead that could only have formed over dry land. The
next sign of land we could see was not land at all, but a band
of green – the tops of palm trees along the shore. They became
distinct before we could see anything under them. Then we
saw black things moving back and forth beneath the trees.
They turned out to be cars driving along the hard sandy beach.
Finally we saw the sand under the cars. The captain had made
a good landfall at the mouth of the St. Johns River.

We lay off the entrance to the river that night and in
the morning a flimsy-looking tug with a tall, skinny stack
came for us. She had the good grace not to belch black coal
smoke over us, but her breath was nearly as unpleasant, being
thick with diesel fumes.

The run up the river was some twenty miles. It felt
strange to be without the roll of the sea underneath. It was
replaced by a new kind of motion – less perceptible to a
landsman, but to a seafarer something like captivity. During

Dis. 1.

CERTIFICATE OF DISCHARGE

FOR A SEAMAN DISCHARGED BEFORE A SUPERINTENDENT OR A CONSULAR OFFICER.

ISSUED BY THE
BOARD OF TRADE.　　**No. 15**

Name of Ship and Official Number, Port of Registry and Gross Tonnage.	Horse Power.	Description of Voyage or Employment.
Sch Jean H Andrus		
La Have N.S		Coastwise

Name of Seaman.		Year of Birth.	Place of Birth.
Charly H Turnbull		1923	Orange N.J

Rank or Rating.	No. of R.N.R. Commission or Certif.	No. of Cert. (if any).
O S		

Date of Engagement.	Place of Engagement.	Copy of Report of Character.*	
		For Ability.	For General Conduct.
13/7/1941	Bridgewater N.S		

Date of Discharge.	Place of Discharge.		
22/8/1941	Jacksonville	O B	O B

I certify that the above particulars are correct and that the above named Seaman was discharged accordingly.

Dated this 20 day of Aug 19 41　　AUTHENTICATED BY

_____ MASTER.　　_____ Signature of Superintendent or Consular Officer

* If the Seaman does not require a Certificate of his character, enter "Endorsement not required" in the spaces provided for the copy of the Report.

Signature of Seaman _____

NOTE.—Any person who forges or fraudulently alters any Certificate or Report, or copy of a Report, or who makes use of any Certificate or Report, or copy of a Report, which is forged or altered or does not belong to him, shall for each such offence be deemed guilty of a misdemeanour, and may be fined or imprisoned.

N.B.—Should this Certificate come into the possession of any person to whom it does not belong, it should be handed to the Superintendent of the nearest Mercantile Marine Office, or be transmitted to the Registrar-General of Shipping and Seamen, Tower Hill, London, E.C.3.

The author's Certificate of Discharge.

this trip we tidied up all the running rigging and enjoyed looking at the new sights of the land. To a landsman it would have been a dull trip. The terrain through which the river flows is flat and lacks all that man classifies as "sights." But we had been deprived of contact with the land for three weeks, and the subtropical vegetation was novel to us. Three weeks of nothing but oceanscape gave us a renewed appreciation of the nonliquid world and bestowed an allure to every thicket, shack and rusting car body.

Our passage ended at a low bulkhead on our starboard side below the city. As soon as we had gotten the mooring lines adjusted the captain got us back to the real world of work and we got the dory over the side. Captain Reid, the vessel's owner, must either have had a love for maroon or he was able to buy a lot of maroon paint at a distress price. We began right away to paint the vessel's dried-out, splintery topsides. The rough spruce planking soaked up the maroon paint as fast as the two met. It looked better than the old black that had grown shabby, but it did not seem as appropriate or as dignified as a new coat of black.

Even the calm of the doldrums, where there was no relief from the dead air and the relentless sun, was cooler than Jacksonville. Just one afternoon of painting the sunny side of the hull had us limp and soaked with sweat. We were almost too uncomfortable to eat supper. Afterward Frenchy, Harry, Ross and I walked up to a little bar a half mile closer to the city. I can never forget the feeling of cool relief as the thin, sharp stream of ice-cold Jax beer slid down my esophagus.

The next morning a man visited the vessel with his son. I assumed that this was the local agent who had made arrangements for the cargo. He wore a white shirt and a tie and looked the proper southern businessman. His son was about my age and had on a slacks suit. This was the latest style for casual wear at that time – slacks, short-sleeved shirt and belt all made from the same cotton cloth. He was clean and had soft hands and his hair was neatly parted. It was obvious that he was curious about the vessel. He seemed to feel awkward and out-of-place. He studied me and I him, neither of us glaring, but communicating in a friendly, nonverbal manner. I had the distinct feeling that our lives had been similar, and that we could easily have been fraternity brothers or even have swapped homes. I knew that he wanted to trade my place on the vessel for his on the shore, at least for a little while. We both knew that he would not. I soon would be returning to the life I had left behind. That life could not have been too different from his. I suspect that he did not want to miss the start of his next semester either. For him a voyage on a tern schooner was an impossible fantasy. For me, the fantasy had turned into reality and was now ended.

That afternoon, 20 August, 1941, the captain took me into the city to the British consulate where I was discharged. The captain paid me my wages in American dollars as well as my bus fare to Saint John, New Brunswick, and my passage across the Bay of Fundy to Digby. He gave me my "ticket" on which he rated me as "very good." A chapter had ended.

The images of expectation had been shattered and replaced by the hard shapes of reality: dreams by discomfort, naivete by firsthand knowledge. I had learned that there is a price for everything. The roll of the deck and clean, sweet air cost me drudgery. The bliss of dolphins under the bow cost me shivering night watches and bleeding hands. The freedom from academia, suburbia, and compliance with parental wishes cost me servitude of a sterner kind. Thinking back from my present vantage point I can see these things and understand these lessons learned and value them. Then I saw only the immediate and the urgent. The romance of Masefield and of countless stirring and nostalgic tales of the sea did not match the realities that I had experienced. The real world did not measure up to the dream world.

But the real world taught lessons that the dream world cannot. Out of struggle can come mastery. Out of the commonplace can come the exceptional. Out of the ordinary man can come nobility. Out of ugliness can come beauty.

Buddhists attach special significance and esteem to the lotus. It is one of the loveliest of flowers and yet its roots lodge in fetid decaying matter on the bottom of stagnant pools. From death and putrefaction it derives life and beauty and gives inspiration and hope to mankind. Lessons and examples are given to us all through life. They often go unheeded for years before being transmuted into profit by maturity.

Ghosts

A load of hard pine was put aboard and the schooner sailed for Bermuda. The lumber was needed for the construction of a United States air base there, but it was never delivered. The following letter to me from Harry gives the story:

Lunenburg, N.S.
February 1st, 1942

Dear Charles,

Sorry to keep you waiting so long. I know you are anxious to hear about the trip.

We left Florida the 29th August – got no one in your place, but we each got a $10 raise. Took storm September 20th about 130 miles from Bermuda, lasted 6-1/2 days; we had to tie ourselves fast for two days and nights; couldn't even sleep. We didn't even save any food – she filled with water so fast, and we fellows trying to get the deck load of lumber off; boats smashed; the jib-boom off (bow-sprit) and the fore-galley washed away, the place where you used to sleep. We were on the wreck 20 days. We used to catch fish (dolphin) and roast them

The *Jean F. Anderson* in port, probably in the 1930s. (M.S.M. 50.2115)

on top of the cabin house, and sometimes eat them raw. We were also out of water for 6 days; made our fish hooks out of door-hooks – I managed to find a file so we could file them down. We used a piece of canvas for bait. We also picked up some small shrimp from the "Gulf Weed" out of the sea. On five days out of the 20 we used to go swimming on the fore-deck (well-deck). Even her break-beam was gone and her fore-companionway from the cabin house was washed away. She was just the same as an accordion – when she moved with the motion of the sea you could see the water squirt through her deck everywhere. That's all that kept her up – the lumber in the holds; even the hatches were washed away.

We saw ships and planes every other day but they wouldn't take any notice of us. They could easily see we were in distress – our sails all gone, expecially the jib-boom, but on the 20th day (Oct. 9th) a British ship picked us off. We were all pretty weak in the legs and we all lost weight – down to between 120 to 130 lbs. They couldn't have treated us any better aboard that British ship – we were aboard her 17 days before we reached Pernambuco (Recife) Brazil.

The Captain, mate and Ross were five weeks before they caught a boat coming North – they went on an American freighter. Frenchie and I were there seven weeks before we could get a boat – we came up on a Brazilian ship, freight and passenger – arrived in New York the day after Christmas. We were there 9 or 10 days before we could get a boat for Halifax. We also stopped at Para and La Guayra, Venezuela, coming up. The British Consul took care of everything.

The Captain and them were home quite a while before I got home – they were even gone again. They are in Boston now to take a boat some place South. Didn't even get any wages yet – can't collect till I see him. We also lost all our belongings on the wreck – saved nothing – no more than what we stood in. Didn't even get your letter from Jamaica. There is even more mail in Bermuda I didn't receive. There's no trouble to get jobs on ships – could have had four or five chances since I'm home – could have even joined one in New York. Frenchie lost that piece of work he was making for your father – he lost everything. I will send you the sea-bean later on. Excuse the bad writing as the pen is very poor.

Your shipmate

Harry

In April 1942, Harry Nauss died of drowning or hypothermia when a rowboat he had borrowed capsized in Halifax Harbor.

In February 1943, Captain St. Clair Geldert died of a heart attack in Yarmouth, Nova Scotia.

Ross Peeler served in combat in World War II with the Canadian infantry in North Africa, Sicily and Italy and twice was severely wounded – shrapnel in the spine. He worked in scallop draggers in the sixties. He was married in 1966 to Verna Mosher and died in Halifax in 1971 of leukemia.

Of Frenchy and the mate, Bill Snow, I have no further information.

As for me, I have been spared and blessed with many good years, good health, one perfect wife, three children, all of whom went to graduate school, and seven grandchildren. After years in the packaging business in the States I retired. Since then I have traveled some and written a lot. I served over three years in the United States Army during World War II because I had grown one inch too tall for the Navy.

Although I remain indebted to my valiant shipmates and to the lessons learned while a sailor before the mast, I rejoice in the wonders and challenges of today.